Writings on
Scholarly Communication

An Annotated Bibliography of Books and Articles on Publishing, Libraries, Scholarly Research, and Related Issues

Herbert C. Morton

Judith Mayers	*Deborah Styles*
Anne J. Price	*Carol Tenopir*
Jane Rosenberg	*Bettina Hagen*

Office of Scholarly Communication and Technology
American Council of Learned Societies
Washington, D.C.

UNIVERSITY
PRESS OF
AMERICA

Copyright © 1988 by

University Press of America,® Inc.

4720 Boston Way
Lanham, MD 20706

3 Henrietta Street
London WC2E 8LU England

All rights reserved

Printed in the United States of America

British Cataloging in Publication Information Available

Co-published by arrangement with
The American Council of Learned Societies

Library of Congress Cataloging-in-Publication Data

Writings on scholarly communication : an annotated bibliography of books and articles
on publishing, libraries, scholarly research, and related issues / Herbert C. Morton . . .
[et al.]. p. cm.
Includes bibliographies and index.
1. Scholarly publishing—Bibliography. 2. Libraries and scholars—Bibliography.
3. Research libraries—Bibliography. 4. Learning and scholarship—Bibliography.
5. Research—Methodology—Bibliography. I. Morton, Herbert C.
Z286.S37W75   1988   016.001—dc 19   87–32931 CIP
ISBN 0–8191–6825–4 (alk. paper)
ISBN 0–8191–6826–2 (pbk. : alk. paper)

Preface

This bibliographic guide is a first approximation, a
provisional effort to suggest the range of material that has been
published on the broad topic of scholarly communication. It seeks
to identify a literature of common interest to scholars,
librarians, publishers, computer specialists, academic
administrators, and others concerned with the advancement of
learning in the humanities and social sciences. Some of the
material and most of the issues are equally relevant to the
concerns of scientists and scholars in professional fields, but
for convenience and manageability, no effort has been made to
include writings in the sciences and professions on the issues
covered in the guide.

The works selected for annotation are intended to be
illustrative rather than definitive. The editors have not
systematically canvassed and assessed the vast literature from
which their selections were drawn. They claim only that these
articles and books are likely to be informative for a wide range
of readers from different backgrounds. The objective was to
identify about one hundred works for lengthy annotations and to
list or annotate briefly an additional one hundred or more. The
approach is discussed in more detail in the Introduction that
follows.

Further exploration and reflection would no doubt lead to the
addition of other books and articles and the deletion of some that
are now included. But we have been encouraged to make available
what we have and leave to a later time the further improvements
that certainly can and will be made. For example, the annotations
were prepared on a computer and ideally ought to be available
online and revised and updated regularly.

The author identifications used throughout are, unless
otherwise specified, affiliations as of the time the work was
published.

Funding for preparation of the bibliography was provided from
grants given by the following organizations for the establishment

of the Office of Scholarly Communication and Technology: the
Andrew Mellon Foundation, the National Endowment for the
Humanities, the Rockefeller Foundation, and the Council on Library
Resources. The office was established in Washington, D.C. in the
fall of 1984 by the American Council of Learned Societies.

June 1987

CONTENTS

INTRODUCTION

Writings on Scholarly Communication

Introduction

by Herbert C. Morton

In the beginning, scholarly communication was simply the act
of Scholar A talking to Scholar B, or Prophet A talking to Prophet
B, or Wise Man A talking to Wise Man B.

But that was long ago, and a couple of millenniums make a
difference. Today, the process is much more complicated, as we
well know. Scholar A still talks to Scholar B, but if he--or
she--has something important to say to others who share the same
interests, he writes a scholarly article or book. If he wants to
know what his colleagues around the country or the world are
doing, he joins professional societies and attends scholarly
meetings, and reads journals. So does she.

Scholars learn, too, that they cannot keep up with all that
is happening by themselves, so they go to the library for help--
for books, for journals, for bibliographies, and for assistance in
searching the online databases.

If they are engaged in research that requires manipulating
large quantitites of data, they go to the computer center for
help--or buy their own computer. If they are in a hurry, they
tie into an electronic mail network.

As they find they need more money to do research and
disseminate their results, they appeal to foundations, government
agencies, and top administrators on campus for help.

And lo and behold, we no longer have simple scholarly
communication, Scholar A talking to Scholar B. We have a system of
scholarly communication involving a large group of players--
scholars, publishers, librarians, computer experts, university
administrators, learned societies, foundations, and government
agencies. And it becomes readily apparent, when you stop to think
about it, that what one group does--decisions about what books to
preserve, journal pricing policies, new technology and copyright,
and so on--often affects the others. The welfare of these groups

groups is inextricably bound together. The theme of
interdependence was the unifying idea in the report of the
National Enquiry into Scholarly Communication in 1979 and a major
reason why the Office of Scholarly Communication and Technology
was established five years later.

If, as the National Enquiry report argued and as many of us
have come to believe, scholarly communication should be viewed as
a system of interdependent groups, it becomes important to try to
understand the characteristics of each of the groups and of the
system by exploring such questions as the following:

What are the concerns of scholars as readers, as users of
libraries and computers, as researchers and as authors?

What is the role of book and journal publishers, what are
trends of production and sales in the publishing industry, and
what are the problems and promises introduced by new technology?

How are libraries adjusting to the increased demands being
made of them as publications continue to proliferate and as new
technology not only imposes new costs and ajustment problems but
also opens up new opportunities to improve library services
generally?

Where do scholarly societies fit in--and also the computer
center directors, the bibliographic utilities and data base
managers, academic administrators, government agencies and
foundations.

Purpose

This bibliography brings together a substantial collection of
material dealing with the many aspects of scholarly communication.
It provides a starting point, a broad perspective on the field
that will enable those who are familiar with one aspect of it to
increase their understanding of other aspects.

Our aim has been to select books and articles in each field
that will be of concern to outsiders. For example, we asked
ourselves what should scholars and publishers know about
developments in the library field? What should scholars and
librarians know about the role of university presses and the
applications of computers in research? These are the kinds of
questions that have guided our selection. We have sought articles
on trends and policy issues that do not delve too deeply into
specialized professional concerns. However, this goal is easier
to state than to reach. Readers may think, justifiably, that in
some instances we have gotten too deeply into professional
concerns.

We make no claim that the selection presented here is either comprehensive or representative. There are gaps in coverage, surely, and no doubt users of this bibliography will, in the realm of their own expertise, second guess our selections. What we do claim instead is that anyone who uses this bibliography will be introduced to a variety of material on important issues related to scholarly communication.

What is distinctive about this bibliography is the length and detail of the annotations, which we hope will prove to be interesting and informative in themselves as well as a guide for further reading.

This bibliography has been assembled in machine readable form, using Nota Bene. It is our hope that the bibliography can be revised and updated and thus become a tool of continuing usefulness.

Summary

The annotations have been grouped under eleven subject headings. Some of the major themes that emerge are summarized below.

Scholarly Communication

The opening section provides an overview of scholarly communication, covering not only the key theme of interdependence, which binds the constituencies together, but also identifying the major issues in the field. Scholarly Communication: The Report of the National Enquiry, the first item, is based on the deliberations of the Board of Governors of the National Enquiry into Scholarly Communication and the research that was carried out to support it over a three-year period. Its three major chapters deal with scholarly journals, books and presses, and research libraries. In each area, major problems are described and analyzed and recommendations are proposed.

May Katzen's article reports on parallel efforts undertaken in Western Europe to explore issues in scholarly communication during the 1970s when American university presses and the American Council of Learned Societies were sponsoring meetings that led to the establishment of the National Enquiry. Katzen's report covers results of information-gathering visits to the United States and several other countries.

Fritz Machlup's ambitious 4-volume study--Information through the Printed Word--was intended to assess the economics of publishing and library operations, but it failed to achieve its objectives largely because it was impossible to obtain good data either from publishers or librarians on the questions he wanted to explore. But it remains a landmark study because of the way Machlup framed the problem and his description of the difficulties encountered in his research. It also contains numerous suggestive findings, though they are often difficult to ferret out.

William Pell's article belongs chronologically with these early publications and will be mentioned here, though the annotation appears in the section devoted to journals. It dealt primarily with the proliferation of journals, circulation, editorial requirements, and financial concerns in the language field, at a time when there was almost nothing else available on these issues. Pell's work was a useful forerunner to the National Enquiry. Collectively, the foregoing publications give a picture of the origins and early development of scholarly communication and many of the central themes.

Two recent publications provide more up-to-date perspectives.

The report on the Survey of Scholars, issued in 1986 by the Office of Scholarly Communication, is annotated in the section on Research and Scholarship but logically warrants mention at this point. It offers a wider view of the terrain than is given in most of the other publications--reflecting, in a sense, the evolution of thinking during the 1980s about the scope of scholarly communication. The original planning for the survey began with a review of a questionnaire developed in the late 1970s by the National Enquiry to ascertain the attitudes of two groups of scholars--a sample of users of scholarly materials and a sample of producers of such materials. Some of the questions on reading habits, authorship, and use of the library are echoed in the much more detailed Survey of Scholars.

In addition, the Survey of Scholars included a large section dealing with applications of computers. What is especially notable is that the Survey of Scholars achieved a response rate of 71 percent, even though the 16-page questionnaire required 30-40 minutes to fill out. This response points to two important conclusions: First, scholars will respond to efforts to obtain information about their concerns and needs, and, second, the issues related to scholarly communication are ones that are of great interest to the scholars in the humanities and social sciences. Among the findings, the criticisms of the peer review process, the acceptance and rapid spread of personal computers in the humanities, and various responses about journals and library use have attracted particular attention.

Complementing the attitudes of scholars on these matters is a statement reflecting the views of librarians. It was issued by the Association of Research Libraries in 1986, entitled "The

Changing System of Scholarly Communication." It is a consensus
statement prepared by the ARL Task Force on Scholarly
Communication. It assesses the problems facing libraries--the
enormous outpouring of publications, budgetary constraints, the
harnessing of new technologies--and sets forth the ARL's
commitment to collaboration with other groups in the advancement
of learning.

Book Publishing

This section is introduced by Elizabeth Eisenstein's
pioneering study of the social transformation brought about by the
introduction of printing. The other works cited offer a broad
view of the publishing industry--describing the history of
publishing, the world of university presses, and how the scholarly
publishing system functions.

Eisenstein's focus is on the way in which printing altered
written communication within the commonwealth of learning. Not
only did printing increase the availability of books, but it made
possible the production of books with identical texts so that the
same information appeared in the same way in different cultures--
an achievement that was to prove enormously important in the
advancement of learning. For those who believe that the
introduction of computer technology is as revolutionary as the
invention of printing, Eisenstein's work can also be viewed as a
historical illustration of how such an innovation becomes "an
agent of change" in society.

The American book industry and the people who work in it is
the subject of a sociological study by Lewis Coser, Charles
Kadushin, and Walter Powell. Heretofore, books about publishing
had usually been written by publishers, editors, and other
insiders. This volume, carefully researched and written for a
nonspecialist audience, offers an outsider's perspective on the
history of the industry, the career patterns of those who work in
it, and the role of the actors in allied fields, such as literary
agents, book reviewers, and so on. Notwithstanding the turmoil in
the industry caused by mergers, the domination of retail
bookstores by big chains, and the introduction of new technology,
the authors remain optimistic about its prospects. The related
reading by Powell offers a first-hand glimpse of manuscript
selection and editorial processes in scholarly publishing.

University presses, whose lists include thousands of titles
each year that would not sell enough copies to interest commercial
publishers, are the subject of a classic study by Chester Kerr.
Written forty years ago (and updated periodically, most recently

in the July 1987 issue of <u>Scholarly Publishing)</u>, it describes the establishment of university presses in the late 19th century and their growth and spread since that time. Kerr's first report explains how the academic publishing sytem works, the relationships between presses and parent universities, and other matters.

One of the great works in the history of scholarship and publishing is the <u>Oxford English Dictionary</u>, a collaborative effort requiring five decades to complete. The story of this project, told by Elizabeth K.M. Murray, granddaughter of the first editor, James A.H. Murray, conveys a deep understanding of the field of lexicography and of the people who were drawn into this exacting, highly controversial, and intensely human enterprise.

The first book-length history of an American university press is the history of the Harvard Press by Max Hall. It provides an informative complement to Kerr's work. Although Harvard did not establish the first university press, it did acquire the first printing press in the colonies. Among Hall's important themes is the dual nature of a press. As an academic institution, it exists to serve scholarship, and as a business enterprise, it must meet the tests of financial prudence and good management, a tension that more than once brought the Harvard press to the brink of disaster. The related readings cite the histories of the Cambridge and Oxford presses, which date back some 500 years, and John Tebbel's one-volume condensation of his four-volume history of American book publishing.

The books by Herbert Bailey and John Dessauer move a step closer to the day-to-day work of publishing. Bailey spells out from a managment perspective how publishing is conducted within a university setting. Dessauer offers a more didactic account of how to publish. For the growing number of scholars, computer in hand, who think of becoming their own publishers, these books offer a broader view of the full demands and opportunities that are implicit in the publisher's job.

Marshall Lee's book on design and production may have a similar relevance. Though it is addressed to the professional, it is easily accessible to the nonspecialist.

The ambitious Library of America program brings to the public the collected works of major American authors in well designed durable editions. At first thought, the project might seem above reproach, entitled to universal approbation. But the manner in which it was handled aroused an angry debate within the publishing community. At stake, according to some of the university presses, was the diversion of subsidies away from the support of scholarly research and publication into the subsidy of book collectors. Of concern also was the competition that the new series would bring to existing university press editions of the same works.

Journal Publishing

The section on journals begins with Charles Osburn's review of the 300-year history of the scholarly journal. Osburn identifies the peer review system as the salient characteristic of the modern journal. It was established to maintain standards of academic quality and to promote the free exchange of research findings and scholarly writing. Although the system has changed little over its first 300 years, the rapid improvement and spread of computer technology has increased the likelihood of substantial changes in the near future. Turoff and Hiltz describe the emergence of four types of electronic publications, ranging from an electronic version of the print-based journal to special publications to suit limited needs.

Anne Piternick looks at the various forms in which journals exist--hard copy, microform, preprints, abstracts, electronic mail, and full text online--and suggests some guidelines for publishers and editors in choosing among these possibilities..

What do readers think of the electronic medium? O.L. Standera reports the results of an experiment in which a journal was produced in three formats--traditional print, microfiche, and electronic. The respondents, faculty members at the University of British Columbia, showed overwhelming preference for the traditional print journal. Cost-benefit estimates also placed the print journal first. A different type of survey seeking to establish journal preferences was conducted for the Royal Society in London. According to J.F.B. Rowland, it also showed (as of the early 1980s) a strong preference among physical and biological scientists for the printed journal over electronic journals.

One of the recommendations of the National Enquiry was that small journals and medium size ones in financial straits should take advantage of economies of scale either by collaboration or by arranging for larger and more efficient publishers to handle their production, marketing, and financial reporting. It was to achieve such efficiencies that the Helen Dwight Reid Foundation established Heldref in the early 1970s. At that time financial pressures were threatening the survival of many good journals. In its first ten years, according to Director Neal Vahle, Heldref took over about forty publications, many of them losing money, and managed to break even or better on the total venture. Since then it has continued to expand.

The broader issue of journal financial management is examined by Mary E. Curtis who has worked both in commercial and nonprofit publishing. She discusses three criteria for measuring journal performance: the quality of the journal itself, its contribution to the journal publication program, and its responsiveness to social and technological change.

Publishing and Technology

The introduction of computer technology in the publishing field has revived old issues and introduced new ones. Irving Horowitz, a sociologist and publisher, and Mary Curtis explore the definition of what will constitute publishing in the electronic age--how publishers will decide what to print, save and discard; and the effects of new technology on copyright and property rights. They analyze the changing roles of scholars, publishers, and librarians in the dissemination process, and they explore the broad social implications of the control of access to computers, photocopying, and information.

Ian Montagnes, the editor of Scholarly Publishing for many years, examined the impact of technology on the major publishing functions, and (as of 1981) found that the effects are greatest in some production and business areas. They are least important in two areas that lie at the heart of publishing: manuscript appraisal and deciding what to publish.

One of the areas in which computers can make a dramatic contribution is editing, especially the editing of special editions and collected works. Michael Groden describes how the computer was used to help edit the corrected edition of Joyce's Ulysses. J.K. McConica and R.M. Schoeffel describe the monumental project of the University of Toronto Press to publish in translation the collected works of Erasmus, which is expected to run to 60 volumes.

In the half-century since the completion of the Oxford English Dictionary, supplementary volumes have been published. Today, the computer (and specially designed software) are being used to integrate the original text, the supplements, and additional new words and revisions. Edmund Weiner, editor of the New Oxford English Dictionary, explains how the project is being carried out and describes Oxford's longer range plans to make the dictionary accessible online after the combined new edition is published. The online version will open up new possibilities for lexicographical study.

Libraries: Role and Prospects

The first two titles in the section on the role and prospects of libraries are explicitly addressed to faculty members and administrators rather than to professional librarians. Arthur Hamlin's comprehensive study of university libraries offers an historical account and a topical treatment of developments in collection building, financing, and the use of new technologies. It provides a setting for the discussions that follows. Barbara Moran focuses on current literature and key issues in library management, with particular emphasis on the importance of comprehensive planning in the face of rapid technological changes.

The collection of essays edited by Thomas Galvin and Beverly Lynch presents an introduction to the current needs of academic libraries. It is addressed to university administrators, and most of the contributors are librarians at major research universities.

Charles Osburn discusses the effect of changing patterns in academic research on library policies. He believes that growing interest in applied research, increased use of informal modes of scholarly communication, and the rise of computer techology have diminished the importance of building comprehensive collections. However, librarians have not adapted their policies to the new research environment. Osburn urges librarians to give greater attention to planning and to cooperative activities.

Several annotations offer different perspectives on the shift from acquisitions and collections to access. Warren J. Haas, president of the Council on Library Resources, attributes the rapidly increasing use of online services and resource sharing to rising library costs, the increasing size of collections, new technology, and changing expectations of users. Together these developments have forced libraries to seek new solutions to access and retrieval problems.

As pointed out in the next article by Gordon Williams-- director of the Center for Research Libraries in Chicago, the "library's library"--it is futile for individual libraries to try to build comprehensive, self-suffucent collections in the face of the recent explosion of knowledge and limited funding. In calling for greater emphasis on cooperation and access, he urges that attention be directed to the library's purpose rather than to its historical means for achieving that purpose.

The central challenge to today's librarians, according to Richard DeGennaro, is managing the transition from collection-centered institutions to ones that provide access. That requires the maintenance of traditional collections and services while automating such operations as cataloging and taking advantage of

new electronic technologies. De Gennaro singles out four major
tasks that are required to provide better support for university
research and instructional needs. Investments to carry out these
tasks cannot be justified on the grounds that in the long run they
will reduce costs--for they will not do so--but rather on the
grounds that they will enable the library to meet the information
services needed in a high technology society.

Patricia Battin believes that university traditions and
structures have deterred the kind of long-range planning that is
needed to take advantage of the new information technology.
Librarians are creating new ways of sharing resources, but the
success of their efforts depends on the ability of the university
community to develop a new structure to provide better access to
knowledge. In this new structure, she envisions a key role for
the library as the unit that historically has built up an
understanding of overall scholarly communication.

Nina Matheson's report on information in the health sciences
suggests that the essential first step in moving forward is to
transform the library "from a repository to an interactive
information transfer and management system" linking every part of
a medical center and tying such centers to other centers and
external information sources. The report's findings have been
viewed as applicable to other libraries, not just medical ones.

The report of a conference of librarians and publishers at
the University of Chicago Graduate Library School highlights the
tensions within each group as it tries to meet conflicting
internal objectives (commercial success, for example, versus
encouragement of creative literature) and the conflicts among the
groups over such issues as copying and pricing, which have been
heightened by new technologies.

In offering a university president's view of the future of
academic libraries, Robert O'Neil urges the deemphasis of
quantitative standards in measuring the performance of a library.
He thinks greater attention should be given to more difficult
factors to measure, such as governance, bibliographic instruction,
professional service, and the protection of intellectual freedom.

The future of the book in the electronic age appears secure
to the Librarian of Congress, Daniel Boorstin. He does not expect
to see online services displace books. The two modes are
complementary, each fulfilling different needs.

Libraries and Computing

In a wide ranging discussion of computer applications to the
field of scholarly communication, Warren J. Haas reviews the

impact of computers on cataloging, indexing, and the dissemination of bibliographic information. These new services do not replace the ones in place but rather complement them and will require continuing high investments that will pose new financial problems for academic institutions. So far computers have not had much effect on delivery of materials, which is still governed by the format in which an item is stored. Many legal and institutional questions have to be settled before new electronic systems of storage, delivery, and use can move ahead.

William Y. Arms offers the perspective of a computer specialist. He sees the university administration assuming a coordinating role to meet the varying needs of scholars, librarians, and managers. He stresses the importance of standardization in making possible the integration of a campus-wide computer system. At the same time the university must retain its flexibility for dealing with changing circumstances.

Computer centers and libraries are providing essentially the same service--delivery of information to the academic community-- according to Lee Jones. Speaking from a library perspective he echoes the plea for integration that Arms made. Among the problems that need to be resolved are inter-organizational rivalries within the library community, library-publisher tensions, telecommunication costs, and copyright conflicts.

Richard McCoy and Wayne Davidson stress the central role that will be played by networks linking the world's major databases. They explain in some detail the use of the database established by the Research Library Group (RLG), which McCoy headed.

The founder of the Online Computer Library Center, Frederick Kilgour, envisions a greatly expanded role for libraries in disseminating information directly to the public with the aid of advanced computer technologies. He describes his work in developing a system called EIDOS (Electronic Information Delivery Online System) that is intended to provide access both to published and unpublished material.

In marked contrast to the other authors cited, F.W. Lancaster and Linda C. Smith, see the eventual replacement of printed information by electronic systems rather than the continuing existence of two complementary systems. The advent of the computer affected secondary systems first, such as abstracting and indexing services, and, in time, will probably transform primary publishing. A decade has passed since Lancaster introduced the concept of the paperless society. An article in 1985 shows that his views have not changed.

What are some of the consequences of increasing dependence on

electronic systems and the gradual phasing out or reduction in the
use of traditional media? Gordon B. Neavill focuses on these
issues, especially the survival of accumulated learning when
information stored in electronic form can easily be altered and
discarded without leaving a trace of the original. He worries
about the possible neglect of the archival function in the
information system and, given the growing role of commercial
database vendors, the retention of information that may not be
financially attractive, such as scholarly works.

A collection of essays edited by E.J. Sigel deals with
practical applications of new technology and speculations about
the future.

Raymond K. Neff deals with a central administrative issue:
the choice between the merger of libraries and computer centers
into a single entity and a collaborative arrangement for more
effective sharing of responsibilities. He describes the strategy
being followed at the University of California-Berkeley which has
a single campus communications network. The library serves as the
academic information system while the computer center provides the
back-up and archiving service.

Online Services

Nearly a decade ago Charles Meadow anticipated many of the
developments in online searching during the 1980s. At a time when
it was widely believed that professional searchers could handle
the task, he argued that searching by the end user would increase,
although there will still be a role for the highly skilled
professional. Strategies for online searching by professional
searchers are explored by Marcia Bates. She identifies twenty-
nine specific tactics based on the literature, her own experience,
and her observation of professional searchers.

Martha Williams offers an introduction to the world of
electronic databases and a comprehensive summary of past, present,
and future issue. One widely debated question is how new
electronic services will be financed. This question is addressed
by Mary Jo Lynch, who reports the results of a survey by the
American Library Association on library financing of online
services. Although the ALA has advocated free access to all
services in public libraries, the survey shows that most libraries
charge for online searching on a cost-recovery basis.

Among the copyright isues that have been given prominence
since the introduction of electronic databases and publishing is
the question of downloading. Thomas Warrick, an attorney,
reviews the legal status of the practice in the light of the

Copyright Act of 1976. Original works in a database are
copyrightable. Downloading is legal if it is consistent with fair
use or carried out by libraries in accord with provisions of the
Copyright Act. Considerable uncertainty remains about some
aspects of the question.

Library Management

A study of library users and circulation data at a medium-
sized academic library leads Paul Metz to conclude that
conventional collection policies are not serving the research
needs of scholars. He believes that library policies are guided
by narrrow interests of some academic departments and unquestioned
beliefs of some librarians rather than by an understanding of user
needs and habits. He notes that there is a wide variation in
research patterns of different users depending upon discipline and
level of expertise. These variations are not taken sufficiently
into account by librarians in building and organizing collections.

One of the keys to improved library service is a better
understanding of user needs and users' assessments of the services
they are getting. In 1983 a committee of the American Library
Association drafted a guide describing several approaches to the
conduct of such studies. It includes a bibliography of examples
of each type of study. A related reading by Herbert S. White
explains why user studies generally have failed. Users have been
conditioned to be satisfied with minimal services and are easily
satisfied. Progress depends on encouraging them to raise their
sights.

The origins and role of the Research Library Group, a
consortium of major libraries organized in 1974, is described by
David Stam. He outlines major problems in developng a unified and
collaborative approach toward national collection development. To
promote the coordination of collections, RLG developed a
Conspectus which serves as a basis for effective national planning
as well a guide for meeting local needs.

Lee Jones views the online catalogue as the most important
force in opening up the use of computers in the library. Surveys
indicate that users respond positively to computerization of
catalogues, although they have been slow to take advantage of
opportunities for bibliographic searching.

The growing emphasis on resource-sharing has encouraged
studies about the effectiveness and costs of interlibrary lending.
The article by Basil Stuart-Stubbs and Denis Richardson focuses on
the pros and cons of using fees for reimbursing lenders.

Ann Okerson assesses patterns in journal pricing and finds

little correlation between the rapid rise in serial prices and the
pace of inflation. Journal prices have risen much faster than the
inflation indexes over the 1970-85 period. They are governed more
by increased production costs, increases in the length of the
average journal, declines in the number of subscribers (which
forces journals to recover their costs from a smaller number of
buyers), and pricing practices such as dual pricing. She thinks
libraries have been too acquiescent in accepting huge increases
and urges them to work together and with publishers to help hold
the increases in check.

The report on library economics by Martin Cummings, former
director of the Library of Medicine is an outgrowth of a two-year
collaborative study supported by the Council on Library Resources.
Building on the work by Baumol and Marcus a decade earlier, it
puts particular emphasis on economic opportunities and problems
arising from the introduction of new technology.

Studies showing the rapid deterioration of books published
since the introduction of acidic paper in the mid-nineteenth
century have greatly increased interest in preservation. Activity
in the mid-1980s includes an effort to dramatize the issue to
scholars, administratators and the public at large. The articles
in Humanities present a nontechnical overview of the situation for
scholars. The three papers on cooperation in preservation
microfilming, which were presented at a meeting of an American
Library Association group, point out that microfilm is still the
best option for preserving the content of printed materials. Very
broad collaboration--not only among library groups but with
scholars, government agencies, and others--is viewed as essential
if the nation's intellectual heritage is to be preserved.

The problem of deciding which records of government to
preserve and which to discard was a central theme of an 18-month
study sponsored by the Council of Library Resources, the American
Council of Learned Societies and the Social Science Research
Council. Among the topics covered were the special problems
arising from the computerization of records.

Computerization of library catalogues usually begins with new
and recent acquisitions and then is gradually extended back to
earlier holdings. "Recon" is the librarian's shorthand for
"retrospective conversion," putting the rest of the entries in the
library card catalogue into an online system. Jutta Reed-Scott,
who conducted a planning study of retrospective conversion for the
Association of Research Libraries discusses the problem and
predicts that by the mid-1990s most of the large research
libraries will have completed the conversion.

Research and Scholarship

Maynard Mack's lecture, inaugurating the ACLS lecture series on "The Life of Learning," includes two sections that are especially appropriate for inclusion in this bibliography. One deals with the overemphasis on campuses today on "published scholarship," which, among other things, encourages seasoned scholars to blow up into mediocre treatises what would have been acceptable essays. The second is the failure to communicate with the community outside the campus, which, in Mack's view, is not only an obligation of the scholar but also much harder work than writing for one's colleagues.

The report on the Survey of Scholars that appears next was noted earlier in this introduction. One aspect of the report worth noting here is that one of six respondents is employed outside the campus--in government, business, research organizations, secondary schools, and so on. These scholars remain very much a part of the academic community, participating in scholarly meetings and other scholarly activities and contributing substantially to the printed literature.

Another major finding of the survey--that about 20 percent of the respondents consider informal publications as important as journal literature--suggests that the so-called invisible college is not just a phenomenon of scientific fields but is becoming increasingly important in the social sciences and humanities as well. Blaise Cronin discusses the development of the invisible college in the sciences and some of its advantages and disadvantages.

Stephen Lock's study of journal peer review--a question of deepening concern in the academic community--is focused chiefly on medical literature, but the issues it raises are applicable to the sciences generally, the social sciences, and the humanities. It is the most informative and comprehensive assessment yet made, covering more than 200 published articles and books. In addition, Lock presents the results of a study of how peer review was carried out at the magazine he edits (The British Medical Journal). He reports the evaluations, decisions on whether to publish, and the ultimate fate (through followup studies) of all the manuscripts received over a six-month period. He thinks peer review is helpful but believes it can be improved.

The article by John Bailar and Kay Patterson complements the Lock study by pointing out the weaknesses of many of the most well known studies of peer review. It also criticizes the scholarly community for its reluctance to investigate a procedure that is so important to academic life. The authors propose a large,

thoroughly coordinated study of how the peer review system is
working.

Academic authorship, like peer review, has been a matter of
concern in the academic community in the 1980s. As president of
Stanford University, Donald Kennedy has been troubled by two
aspects of the matter: proper credit for the efforts of young
faculty and graduate students who are part of research teams and
the proliferation in the number of authors whose names are
typically attached to published articles. He offers suggestions
for establishing guidelines to govern these matters.

Traditionally, preservation has been a job for librarians,
and in this bibliography it is treated under the heading of
library management. But a notable experiment by the American
Philological Association bears mention here. It is the first
effort by a scholarly society to take a major responsibility for
preserving much of its own literature. The article by Roger
Bagnall and Carolyn Harris recounts how the study was conducted
and what its results were. It also discusses the special reasons
why the approach worked in the field of classics but is not
generally applicable. The report illustrates the potential role
of scholars in the preservation effort and the difficulty of
reaching a consensus within a discipline on what to save and what
to discard.

Eleanor Harmon's article on manuscript editing is addressed
primarily to editors, but it should prove equally illuminating to
scholars who are curious about how a first-rate editor sizes up
her role and responsibilities. The related reading complements
Harmon's article by dealing explicitly with editor-author
relationships.

Scholars and Technology

Between 1974 and 1984 the personal computer business grew
from a cottage industry to a multi-billion-dollar industry.
David Ahl, the founder of Creative Computing, offers an anecdotal
account of the major dvelopments during this decade of growth,
such as the creation of Apple I in 1976, the transition from kits
to packaged systems, and the arrival of the IBM PC in 1981. By
the end of this ten-year period, the personal computer had become
a basic tool for business, education and research.

Among the many guides that sought to introduce potential
users to the personal computer was one prepared for the
Heath/Zenith Z-100 by Hugh Kenner, professor of English at the
Johns Hopkins University. Kenner, a noted scholars and writer,
was one of the early converts to the computer and one of the first

to perceive its enormous potential for scholars in the humanities.
His presentation is clear, entertaining, and instructive. It
covers how computers operate, why there are different programming
languages, how software works, and the uses of wordprocessing and
other programs.

Keeping up with the rapid growth and change in the database
market and the microcomputer industry would be an impossible task
for the user were it not for reference books such as those
published by Cuadra Associates and R.R. Bowker Company. Cuadra's
Directory of Online Databases describes the offerings of more than
350 vendors and explains the conditions under which they are made
available. It is updated every six months. Bowker's 1987
directory covers 23,000 organizations in the microcomputing
industry--manufacturers and distributors of equipment, software
publishers and distributors, periodicals, associations and so on.

A byproduct of the use of computers by humanists has been the
creation of data banks--large ones such as the Thesaurus Linguae
Graecae (TLG), which is intended for use by the discipline, and
smaller ones created for specific research purposes of individual
scholars but that may also be useful to other scholars. Theodore
Brunner, who developed TLG, draws lessons from his experience that
he hopes will be useful to his colleagues in the humanities.

Joseph Raben, an early leader in the application of computers
in the humanities, explores the potential usefulness of these new
research tools and discusses how they are likely to alter the way
scholars conduct their research.

To keep the library and scholarly community abreast of
developments in the optical disk field, the Fred Meyer Charitable
Trust commissioned a series of reports. The three cited here,
written by David C. Miller, describe the kinds of disks available,
their capabilities and uses, and their limitations.

The use of a Kurzweil scanner in preparing a special edition
of Thomas Carlyle's works is described in an article on optical
scanners that appeared in Scholarly Communication. Computers made
it possible to compare several editions of each of the Carlyle
volumes that had been retrieved by scanning, thereby contributing
to the publication of a more definitive edition.

John Shelton Lawrence's book is intended to show scholars who
are familiar with personal computers how to use them more
effectively in research, instruction, and administrative tasks.
It covers such topics as the use of computers in electronic
communication, in collaborative and team writing, electronic
filing, searching for information, and electronic publishing.

ARRAS is a versatile computer program for the analysis of
texts. It can, for example, display each occurrence of a word or

categories of words. It enables users to trace historical
developments over a large database of texts by showing patterns,
themes, stylistic traits, grammatical forms and other features.
One of its major applications has been retrieval and analysis of
text in the ARTFL project (American and French Research on the
Treasury of the French Language) at the University of Chicago.
Originally designed by John B. Smith for a mainframe computer,
ARRAS is also available in a version for microcomputers.

Pamela McCorduck offers an historical, philosophical, and
moral discussion of the subject of artificial intelligence, from
Charles Babbage's analytical engine to the late 1970s. A novelist
with a great enthusiasm for research in this burgeoning field, she
is a careful researcher and a gifted communicator. In contrast to
Joseph Weizenbaum, a pioneering computer scientist, she seems
untroubled by the implications of new technology. Weizenbaum,
whose book appeared three years earlier, warns against the dangers
of pursuing computer applications just because they are
technically possible. He argues that new technologies should not
be allowed to progress faster than the ethical and philosophical
understanding that is necessary to make sure that they are used
for the common good. Though much of Weizenbaum's book is too
technical for the average scholar, the discussion of ethical and
policy issues is clearly and simply expressed and reveals a rare
blend of scientific understanding and humanistic sensibilities.

Policy: Copyright, Funding, Access

In 1986 the Office of Technology Assessment completed a
lengthy report on the effect of information and communication
technologies on the intellectual property system. It focuses on
the copyright system and covers the constitutional basis for
property rights, economic issues and such questions as the federal
role in administering these rights. The OTA sees not only a need
to move on some matters at the present time but also the need to
prepare to act again within the decade in order to keep up with
ongoing and significant changes.

The articles that are cited next deal in greater detail with
copyright policy, privatization of federal data, and limitations
on access. Dennis McDonald's review of copyright issues focuses
on how payments should be made for the use of copyrighted work and
assesses such alternatives as taxation of copy equipment and
distributing the proceeds on the basis of sampling procedure and
price discrimination. Related readings deal with library and
publisher attitudes toward copyright.

Peter Hernon and Charles McClure review the effect of government policies during the 1980s on public access to public information. They are troubled by cutbacks in government publication programs, the shift of responsibility for publishing government information to the private sector, cuts in federal funding of libraries, and tighter security on government documents. These all serve to diminish the public's access to important information.

Paul Starr and Ross Corson discuss access to government data from a broader historical, philosophical, and social perspective. They, too, are especially concerned that privatization of government information will make access more costly and limit the availability of public data to those who can afford to pay for it. Moreover, they fear that so-called unprofitable data would not be made available at all if decisions on what to save and make available are dictated primarily by economic criteria. They single out several fields in which the free flow of government information is especially important, such as medical research, higher education, and economic reform.

The conflict between the tradition of academic freedom and the need to protect national security is John Shattuck's central theme. He gives particular attention to the requirements for prepublication review of government sponsored university research, controls on the flow of sensitive but unclassified information, and the refusal of the federal government to allow foreign nationals with controversial views to enter the United States to fill speaking engagements.

Concluding Remarks

It has been said, with some justification, that the concept of scholarly communication is vague and difficult to grasp. Yet as soon as the talk turns to specifics, doubt and indifference vanish. There is not much question about the relevance or significance of the fairness of peer review, funding requirements for research and libraries, prices of scholarly journals, sharing information on new computer applications, preservation of deteriorating materials, better access to the vast and rapidly growing heritage of scholarship, trends in government information policy, and so on.

In preparing this bibliography, we have sought not only to indicate by our selections the breadth of activities suggested by the term scholarly communication but also to demonstrate that the term embraces specifics that permit investigation, analysis, and discussion.

Each of these specific issues is itself a sufficient field of study. Why make thinking about it even more complicated by linking them all together? The answer is that they are linked by their nature. Thinking about each in isolation is an important and necessary task, but it does not break the link. At some point, after exploring each question in itself, an academic administrator must weigh funds for some group or some purpose against alternative claimants. At many points the scholar's world and the librarian's concerns overlap. The great theme of discussions in the library field for a decade or more has been: Think about access not just about holdings and acquisitions. Yet this notion, which has great implications for the way scholars work, has hardly begun to penetrate their thinking--largely because librarians and scholars are not in the habit of spending much time together or looking at what the other is reading. These are not isolated examples.

Few of the works cited in this bibliography refer directly to "scholarly communication." Scholarly communication is the idea that reminds us of the interconnections and the need to consider the consequences for others of decisions made in specific fields. It may still begin with Scholar A talking with Scholar B, but it does not end there, as these writings attest.

BIBLIOGRAPHY

I

SCHOLARLY COMMUNICATION

Scholarly Communication: The Report of the National Enquiry
Trends in Scholarly Communication in the United States and Western
    Europe by MAY KATZEN.
"The Changing System of Scholarly Communication"
    by the ARL Task Force on Scholarly Communication.
Information through the Printed Word: The Dissemination of
    Scholarly, Scientific. and Intellectual Knowledge
    by FRITZ MACHLUP, KENNETH LEESON, and Associates

Related reading

"Two Cheers for the National Enquiry: A Partial Dissent"
    by AUGUST FRUGE.
"The National Enquiry and its Critics" by BERNARD GOLDMAN,
    DAVID BARTLETT, MARILYN GAULL, and AUGUST FRUGE.
The Future of Scholarly Communication: Minutes of the Ninety Fifth
    Meeting by the Association of Research Libraries.
Scholarly Communication in Transition" by JACK MEADOWS.
Communicating Ideas: The Crisis of Publishing in a Post-Industrial
    Society by IRVING LOUIS HOROWITZ.

Scholarly Communication: The Report of the National Enquiry.
Baltimore: The Johns Hopkins University Press, 1979.

This study was initiated during the middle 1970s following a
series of meetings to discuss what appeared to be an impending
crisis facing publishers, libraries, and others trying to cope
with major economic and technological changes. The final report,
drafted for the Board of Governors of the National Enquiry by
David Breneman and Herbert C. Morton, concludes that there was a
"need to redefine the crisis as less dramatic than was earlier
thought, but more persistent and difficult to handle." It
stresses that quantitative changes have taken place in the
scholarly enterprise that require qualitative changes in the
methods of scholarly communication. The report presents a dozen
recommendations in an opening "Overview" chapter and additional
recommendations on the specific topics treated in three succeeding
chapters, which are devoted to scholarly journals, scholarly books
and presses, and research libraries. One of the recommendations
proposed establishment of a permanent Office of Scholarly
Communication. It was this recommendation that led ACLS to open
an Office of Scholarly Communication.

The unifying theme of the report, as stated in the Preface by
R. M. Lumiansky, president of the American Council of Learned
Societies, which sponsored the study: "During the period of the
Enquiry we came to realize more clearly than any of us had earlier
realized the truth of one axiom: the various constituencies
involved in scholarly communication--the scholars themselves, the
publishers of books and of learned journals, the research
librarians, the learned societies--all are components of a single
system and are thus fundamentally dependent upon each other."

Related reading

Fruge, August. "Two Cheers for the National Enquiry: A Partial
Dissent." Scholarly Publishing 10 (April 1979): 211-18. A member
of the board of the National Enquiry, Fruge concentrates his
criticism on the recommendation to establish a National Periodical
Center, the most controversial proposal in the report that was
also widely opposed by the information industry and journal
editors.

Goldman, Bernard, David Bartlett, Marilyn Gaull, and August Fruge.
"The National Enquiry and its Critics." Book Forum, special
issue, vol. 5 (1979). Four highly critical views of the Enquiry
following the presentation of excerpts from the report itself.

Association of Research Libraries. The Future of Scholarly
Communication: Minutes of the Ninety Fifth Meeting, October 17-18,
1979. Washington, 1980.

KATZEN, MAY. Trends in Scholarly Communication in the United
States and Western Europe. University of Leicester, Primary
Communications Research Centre, March 15, 1978.

This report presents the results of one of the first projects
by the Primary Communications Research Centre established by the
British Library Research and Development Department. The Centre
was founded to promote communication and research on the
generation, production, storage and transfer of research
information, a mission closely related to that of the ACLS Office
of Scholarly Communication.

The report summarizes the results of information-gathering
visits to the United States, France, the Netherlands, Luxembourg,
the German Federal Republic, Jerusalem and Scandinavia. Drawing
on the findings, Katzen provides a picture of perceptions about
libraries and publication systems during the late 1970s. She
emphasizes the growing tendency to perceive information as a vital
social resource and a basic component of the decision making
process. It is important to note that although many observers
believe that the problems are rooted in the economic crisis of the
1970s, economic difficulties simply highlighted fundamental
transformations in the scale and pattern of information production
and dissemination. The great increase in scholarly productivity
from the late 1950s onward placed greater demands upon libraries.
The inability of single institutions to respond to all these
demands both stressed the existing cooperative systems and gave
rise to new ventures. Growing cooperation among libraries led to
friction with publishers, since photocopying increased greatly.
More rapid dissemination by computers would bypass the expensive
and unwieldy publications process, but the expense would require
new sources of funds, and numerous legal and technological
questions have not been resolved. While some of the details
relate to plans and activities that have long since been
superseded, this report is still important as a baseline document.

Katzen is director of the Office of Humanities Communication
at Leicester.

Related reading

Meadows, Jack. "Scholarly Communication in Transition." Journal
of Information Science 7 (1983): 81-97. This is the report of a
workshop organized by the Primary Communications Research Centre
and held April 28-29, 1983. Participants explored the interaction
between print and electronic media in relation to trends in
scholarly communication. The papers were written by librarians,
publishers, and information vendors, and represent a variety of
views on the future of scholarly communication.

ARL Task Force on Scholarly Communication. "The Changing System of Scholarly Communication." Washington: Association of Research Libraries, March 1986.

This statement was issued "to present the perceptions held within the research library community about changes taking place in the scholarly communication system and to stimulate dialogue among the major participants in the system."

It discusses first the technological changes that have enabled libraries to make important advances in storing information and making it more accessible to scholars. Those changes have also placed new burdens on libraries to train more specialized staff and to find additional sources of funds. To a large extent the library's historical role has been "reactive", but nonetheless highly important in the scholarly communication process. However, their recent efforts at cooperation--visible in the work of the Association of Research Libraries, the Center for Research Libraries, regional research library organizations, the Research Libraries Group, OCLC, and others--"demonstrate that librarians are more acutely aware of the changing environment than are the scholarly communities they serve and to which they are accountable."

The increase in the number of active scholars "has seriously overloaded" the system and a "flood of communication has affected quality control" and "increased the propensity to state intellectual claims by rushing to print." New technology "is contributing directly and indiscriminately to the productivity of scholars." The extent to which scholarship has been changed and the implications for libraries are still not clear. The relationship between the libraries and scholars is not as close as would be desirable.

Much more needs to be learned about the "information-seeking behavior of scholars" and vigilance is needed in the face of governments and other activities that may adversely affect the free flow of information.

In conclusion, the statement says that the "ARL will align itself aggressively with other system participants to help guide development of the international scholarly communication system in the interests of scholarship."

Related reading

Horowitz, Irving Louis. Communicating Ideas: The Crisis of Publishing in a Post-Industrial Society. Oxford: Oxford University Press, 1986. A wide-ranging collection of essays from a sociologist's perspective.

MACHLUP, FRITZ, KENNETH LEESON and Associates. Information through the Printed Word: The Dissemination of Scholarly, Scientific, and Intellectual Knowledge. 4 vols. New York: Praeger, 1978 and 1980.

This ambitious study under the direction of the economist who pioneered in the analysis of the knowledge sector of the economy, is instructive more for its breadth, conceptual approach, and methodological rigor than for its success in achieving its objective. Titles of its four volumes--Book Publishing, Journals, Libraries and Books, Journals and Bibliographic Services--indicate its scope. The authors are exemplary in explaining their research approach and the difficulties to be overcome. They are also scrupulous in pointing out the limitations of their data. For the most part the data are fragmentary and inconclusive, owing primarily to the difficulty of obtaining comparable information from the major constituencies--book and journal publishers, and libraries. Indeed, an unintended contribution of the study is its demonstration of the difficulty of assembling data in areas where record-keeping varies greatly among organizations and where data are often kept in a form that is not suitable for economic analysis. For example, despite the willingness of publishers in the sample to cooperate, Machlup could not obtain the data he sought. Sales data were usually available only by dollars, not units; hardbound and paperback sales by title were not kept separate; few publishers kept data by field of interest, and those that did used their own definitions, not an established standard.

Notwithstanding its limitations, the study does present a number of interesting findings. These include tabular material in volume 4 comparing the performance of university presses and commercial publishers of serious nonfiction based on cohort analysis. (Books published in 1968 are one cohort, books published in 1969 another, and so on.) This analysis of eleven university presses and nine commercial publishers indicates that commercial publishers make more money because they print titles that appeal to a larger market (longer press runs mean lower costs per volume). They also use higher markups and lower discounts. On a key question of interest to economists, the authors find evidence of vigorous competition in both the journal and book markets. Neither field is dominated by a single publisher or handful of publishers.

The study of libraries in volume 3 is beset with the same difficulties encountered in the other areas, but it, too, reports some useful findings. For example, a survey of steps taken to cut periodical costs show that the most important are dropping duplicate subscriptions and adding fewer subscriptions. Libraries also shifted some of the book budget to the purchase of periodicals.

Overall, this is an indispensable study for anyone interested in conducting research in the field, but it requires patience and persistence as the results are not integrated and no index is provided.

II

BOOK PUBLISHING

The Printing Press as an Agent of Change: Communications and
        Cultural Transformation in Early-Modern Europe
        by ELIZABETH L. EISENSTEIN.
Books: The Culture and Commerce of Publishing
        by LEWIS A. COSER, CHARLES KADUSHIN, and WALTER W. POWELL.
A Report on American University Presses by CHESTER KERR
Caught in the Web of Words: James A. H. Murray and the Oxford
        English Dictionary by K. M. ELISABETH MURRAY.
Harvard University Press: A History by MAX HALL.
The Art and Science of Book Publishing by HERBERT S. BAILEY JR.
Book Publishing: What It Is, What It Does by JOHN DESSAUER.
Bookmaking: The Illustrated Guide to Design by MARSHALL LEE.
"Aiming the Canon" by DAVID J. NORDLOH.

Related reading

A Short History of the Printed Word by WARREN CHAPPEL
Books and Society in History: Papers of the Association of College
        and Research Libraries Rare Books and Manuscripts
        Preconference edited by KENNETH CARPENTER.
Medieval Technology and Social Change by LYNN WHITE, JR.
Getting into Print: The Decision-Making Process in Scholarly
        Publishing by WALTER W. POWELL.
The University as Publisher edited by ELEANOR HARMAN.
To Advance Knowledge: A Handbook on American University Press
        Publishing by GENE R. HAWES.
"What is a University Press?"
        by SHELDON MEYER and LESLIE E. PHILABAUM.
The English Language by ROBERT BURCHFIELD.
"Publishing the Plan of St. Gall" by JAMES CLARK.
The Oxford University Press: An Informal History
        by PETER SUTCLIFFE.
Between Covers: The Rise and Transformation of American Book
        Publishing by JOHN TEBBEL.
Cambridge University Press, 1584-1894 by M. H. BLACK.
What Happens in Book Publishing edited by CHANDLER GRANNIS.
Methods of Book Design: The Practice of an Industrial Craft
        by HUGH WILLIAMSON.
"HBJ to Publish 50-volume America's Library by 1985"
        from Publisher's Weekly.
"Classics by the Pound" by HUGH KENNER.

EISENSTEIN, ELIZABETH L. The Printing Press as an Agent of
Change: Communications and Cultural Transformation in Early-Modern
Europe. Cambridge: Cambridge University Press, two volumes,
1979. Paperback edition, 1980, in one volume. Abridged edition,
The Printing Revolution in Early Modern Europe, 1980.

This is a pioneering scholarly work exploring the long
neglected subject of the "unacknowledged revolution" that resulted
from the advent of printing in the fifteenth century. Eisenstein
views printing--the printers themselves as well as the new
technology--as an agent of change that transformed Western
culture. While acknowledging the enormous role of printing in
increasing literacy, Eisenstein is primarily interested in the way
in which "printing altered written communication within the
Commonwealth of Learning"--the methods of data collection, storage
and retrieval systems and communications networks used by learned
communities throughout Europe in the fifteenth and sixteenth
centuries. Rapid duplication made materials much more widely
available and gradually halted the corruption of texts by scribes,
(though the first printed works served to perpetuate them).
Uniformity of texts in all printed copies encouraged the
development of alphabetical indexes. The author stresses the
importance, for the advancement of learning, of having identical
data available in identical form in different cultures. Images
bearing identical labels enabled astronomers, geographers,
botanists and zoologists to expand their data beyond previous
experience. Classsical learning was revived. Students who took
full advantage of printed texts, which served as "silent
instructors," were less likely to defer to traditional authority
and were more receptive to new ideas. Communications were altered
by the closer association of printers with professors and
merchants. The printer's role was especially significant because
it was he who decided what to publish, the number of copies to
print, and how and where to sell them. From the early emphasis on
theology and school books, they increasingly turned to the
publication of classical texts, Reformation works, and science.

Eisenstein is professor of history, Michigan State
University.

Related reading

Chappel, Warren. A Short History of the Printed Word. New York:
Alfred A. Knopf, 1970. Paperback, Boston: David R. Godine, 1980.
The history of printing as an art, a trade, and a medium of
communication. Superbly illustrated.

Carpenter, Kenneth, ed. Books and Society in History: Papers of
the Association of College and Research Libraries Rare Books and
Manuscripts Preconference. New York and London: R. R. Bowker Co.,
1983.

White, Lynn, Jr. Medieval Technology and Social Change. Oxford:
Oxford University Press, rev. ed. 1967.

COSER, LEWIS A., CHARLES KADUSHIN and WALTER W. POWELL. Books: The Culture and Commerce of Publishing. New York: Basic Books, 1982.

This is a rare outsider's view of the book industry written from the perspective of sociologists. It focuses on the history and structure of publishing, the roles and career patterns of those who work in it, and the functions of those in allied fields (literary agents, book reviewers and book sellers). To keep their study within manageable limits, the authors have chosen to exclude fiction from their inquiry, as well as such publishing concerns as copyright, book manufacturing, and computer technology. It is a highly informative and well written book that will interest anyone with a curiosity about how the book business works.

As sociologists, the authors say their perspective differs from that of others (such as economists) because they are especially "attentive to the personal and organizational relations that nourish books." They illuminate these relationships by drawing on sample surveys, interviews and first-hand observations of people at work. They explore the role of personal networks in transferring information. Ties are found to be very close among scholarly editors, less close among trade book editors. Formal channels of manuscript submission are shown to be much less useful than informal ones and should be a last resort.

On balance, the authors are optimistic about the future of book publishing, notwithstanding the takeovers of independent publishing houses by conglomerates, the insanity of the multimillion dollar bidding for paperback rights, and the increasing domination of book selling by chain stores. These developments, which have been unusually visible in recent years, are hardly unprecedented, the authors point out, and don't presage serious difficulties for the industry.

Coser is distinguished professor of sociology at SUNY, Stony Brook. Kadushin is professor of sociology at the Graduate Center, CUNY. Powell is associate professor of behavior and management and sociology at Yale.

Related reading

Powell, Walter W. Getting into Print: The Decision-Making Process in Scholarly Publishing. Chicago: The University of Chicago Press, 1985. This detailed case study of manuscript selection, editorial processes, and publishing decisions in two firms complements the Coser, Kadushin and Powell work described above. It is an uneven study, excellent in its first-hand descriptions of the practices of the firms under observation but tedious and unsatisfying in its efforts to put these studies in the broader context of the literature of organizational development and management.

KERR, CHESTER. A Report on American University Presses. Chapel Hill, N.C.: The University of North Carolina Press, 1949.

For anyone interested in learning about university presses, this widely cited study is the place to start. It is based on a survey conducted in 1948 and 1949 under the sponsorship of the American Council of Learned Societies, with a grant from the Rockefeller Foundation. In eighteen chapters, Kerr systematically discusses the nature of the university press, its early history, the relations of the press with its parent university and with the scholar, the staffing and management of the press, and decision making on such matters as what to publish, book production, distribution choices, nonbook activities, financial management, cooperation among presses--and finally a judicious set of "Personal Opinions".

The first American university press in continuous operation was established, as Kerr points out, at the Johns Hopkins University Press in 1878 (four centuries after the founding of the Oxford University Press). The rationale stated by the university president, Daniel Coit Gilman, remains the essential statement of the purpose of university publishing: "It is one of the noblest duties of a university to advance knowledge and to diffuse it not merely to those who can attend daily lectures, but far and wide."

Kerr published a supplement to his report in 1955, and in October 1969, for the first issue of the new quarterly Scholarly Publishing, he updated the story in "The Kerr Report Revisited."

Related reading

Harman, Eleanor, editor. The University as Publisher. Toronto: University of Toronto Press, 1961. A book of essays on all aspects of university publishing, written for scholars and the public to mark the seventy-fifth anniversary of the first press established in Canada.

Hawes, Gene R. To Advance Knowledge: A Handbook on American University Press Publishing. New York: Association of American University Presses, 1967.

Meyer, Sheldon and Leslie E. Philabaum, "What is a University Press?" Scholarly Publishing 11 (April 1980) 213-19. A restatement of the role, problems, and achievements of university presses by the senior vice president of the Oxford University Press, New York, and the director of the Louisiana State University Press. They stress that "the single greatest problem facing university presses today and tomorrow is financing. Scholarly publishing is subsidized publishing...Many of the best, most important, and most enduring scholarly books have never sold sufficient copies to pay the costs of their publication."

MURRAY, K. M. ELISABETH. Caught in the Web of Words: James A. H. Murray and the Oxford English Dictionary. New Haven and London: Yale University Press, 1977.

The compilation and publication of the Oxford English Dictionary is clearly one of the great scholarly achievements of the past century. Though it was an enormous collaborative effort extending over five decades, it was the leadership of its senior editor, James A. H. Murray, that got the job done against heavy odds and that assured the dictionary's quality and its enduring reputation as the most important work of historical lexicography in English. This biography by his granddaughter catches the spirit of Murray at work. It shows the difficult intellectual and managerial problems that confronted him and the courage, commitment, and exceptional intelligence, that were required for the project to succeed.

The singular contribution of Murray and his colleagues was the application of the historical method, tracing the life history of every word included and avoiding the conjectural etymologies that had been typical. Murray fully recognized the growing and changing nature of the language in contrast to predecessors, such as Samuel Johnson, who viewed the dictionary as an instrument for establishing a standard of good literary English.

Related reading

Burchfield, Robert. The English Language. New York: Oxford University Press, 1985. The chief editor of the four volume Supplement to the Oxford English Dictionary provides an insightful and readable introduction to the nature, origin, and development of the language.

Clark, James. "Publishing the Plan of St. Gall." Scholarly Publishing 13 (January 1982): 101-17. A brief fascinating account of an unusual achievement in scholarly publishing that echoes some of the personality clashes of the Murray story, though it deals with an entirely different kind of scholarly work.

HALL, MAX. <u>Harvard University Press: A History.</u> Cambridge, Mass.: Harvard University Press, 1986.

This is the first book-length history of an American university press, and it merits a place alongside the histories of the British university presses, Oxford and Cambridge.

Harvard owned and operated the first printing press to be brought to the American colonies, and from the early 1640s on it published intermittently an assortment of broadsides, books and other materials. The Harvard University Press, in its present form, however, was not established until 1913.

Publication of the history came at a time of high achievement and prosperity for the press, which has not always enjoyed either security or success. Indeed, Hall's history ends in 1972, at a difficult moment in the history of the press, which along with other university presses had been caught in an abrupt slump in sales.

Over the years, internal as well as external pressures contributed to the problems. One internal difficulty was the need to make others understand the unique dual role of a university press, which is both an academic institution and a business enterprise. It exists to serve scholarship--to disseminate scholarly works that would not sell enough copies to warrant commercial publication--but it must also meet tests of financial prudence and good management. The biggest threat to the future of the press came during the presidency of James B. Conant who, until late in his administration, saw little use for a university press and once proposed having a commercial firm publish Harvard's books. But strong support from some key faculty members and the determination of Roger L. Scaife, the fourth director, enabled the press to survive. It reached new heights under the fifth director Thomas L. Wilson. Under his stewardship from 1947-67 the press also gained a measure of financial durability from the grant that established the Belknap Press of Harvard University Press. Wilson was succeeded by Mark Carroll, and, in turn, he was succeeded by Arthur J. Rosenthal, who commissioned the volume. The story ends with his appointment in 1972.

Related reading

Sutcliffe, Peter. <u>The Oxford University Press: An Informal History.</u> Oxford: Clarendon Press, 1978. This volume marks the 500th anniversary of printing at Oxford University. It deals mostly with the period since 1860 when the OUP achieved its position as an international publisher of works for general readers as well as scholars.

Black, M.H. <u>Cambridge University Press, 1584-1894</u>. Cambridge, London and New York: Cambrdige University Press, 1984.

Tebbel, John. <u>Between Covers: The Rise and Transformation of American Book Publishing.</u> New York: Oxford University Press, 1987.

BAILEY, HERBERT S. Jr. <u>The Art and Science of Book Publishing</u>.
New York: Harper and Row, 1970. Paperback, Austin: University of
Texas Press, 1980.

DESSAUER, JOHN. <u>Book Publishing: What It Is, What It Does</u>. New
York: R. R. Bowker, 1974. Second edition, 1981.

These two surveys of book publishing cover some similar
ground and have both been widely used in publishing courses, but
they differ in emphasis and style. Bailey has written a more
analytical book and a more personal one, drawing on his experience
as director of the Princeton University Press. Though it is
primarily a descriptive, prescriptive and pragmatic view of the
management of a publishing enterprise, it also reflects the
author's strong sense of commitment. But it is the role of the
publisher "as the manager of the publishing house" that concerns
him, rather than the role as editor and list builder. His three
key chapters deal with work flows, sequences and decisions (from
inviting an author to submit a manuscript to final publication
decisions), the economics of micro publishing (decisions about the
individual book) and planning (short range and long range). A
chapter on the new technologies, though written in 1970, remains
sensible and remarkably up-to-date, pointing out both what new
technology will not be able to do (replace the author, editorial
judgment and marketing imagination--or the book) and what changes
it will be able to bring about through the sharing of resources by
electronic means and the introduction of printing in the home by
machines that capture what is being shown on the video screen.

Dessauer has written a more systematic and didactic volume
that begins with the historical development of publishing and
continues with chapters on editing, manufacturing, marketing,
storage and delivery, and planning. His scope is broader than
Bailey's, since he is interested in describing in comparable
fashion each of the major publishing functions in contrast to
Bailey's focus on management. He also deals with such issues as
copyright and censorship.

Bailey was director of the Princeton University Press for 32
years before retiring in 1986. Dessauer, a university publisher
for many years, has written regularly for <u>Publishers Weekly</u> on the
economics of publishing and is director of the Center for Book
Research at the University of Scranton.

Related reading

Grannis, Chandler, editor. <u>What Happens in Book Publishing</u>. New
York: Columbia University Press, 1957. Second edition, 1967. A
survey of operations in the publishing world written by leading
practitioners.

LEE, MARSHALL.   Bookmaking: The Illustrated Guide to Design,
Production, Editing. Second edition. New York: R. R. Bowker,
1979.

   Attractive, instructive and handy, this book for designers
and production editors may interest a wider audience now that more
authors and others are becoming directly engaged in the production
of publications through their use of personal computers and
desktop publishing equipment. Not that they would need to know
much of what is contained in this widely consulted book, but their
interest may be whetted simply because they have been made aware
of what is involved in the design and production of printed
material. The book is well written and reflects the rich
experience of a designer who has had a long and distinguished
career.

   The work is comprehensive, providing an introduction to the
history and functions of bookmaking, systematic descriptions of
the production technologies (composition, typography, plates and
printing, paper, and so on). It also proceeds step-by-step
through the designing process from the analysis of the manuscript
to the specific elements of design. The illustrations are
excellent and very helpful. The second edition includes a new
section on editing and editorial considerations.

                         Related reading

Williamson, Hugh.   Methods of Book Design: The Practice of an
Industrial Craft. Third edition. New Haven: Yale University
Press, 1983. More sharply focused on questions of design than
Marshall Lee's book, the first edition of this work, which was
focused on British practice, appeared earlier and has become
recognized as an indispensable book for designers. The third
edition has been substantially rewritten to take into account new
technology and its implications for design. Williamson gives
particular attention to differences in type faces and to
variations in the metal and film versions of the same face.

NORDLOH, DAVID J. "Aiming the Canon." Scholarly Publishing 16
(January 1985): 109-19.

The Library of America--a nonprofit publishing project begun
in 1979--issued its first titles in 1982 and in the mid-1980s was
adhering to its original schedule of producing eight titles a year
of the collected works of major American writers. While the
project may be judged successful by almost every criterion of
serious publishing, some of the university presses which have
produced full scholarly editions of titles offered in the series,
are irate. This article offers a full explanation of the reasons
for their ire, describes the differences in the publishing goals
of the Library and the scholarly presses, and warns of the dangers
inherent in the enterprise.

The debate goes beyond professional jealousy. The generously
funded Library of America, sells its books by mail through an
arrangement with Time-Life books and in bookstores through
arrangement with Viking; university presses must rely on small
sales staffs and catalogs to promote their books among scholars
and libraries. The Library is essentially a reprint series; the
university presses emphasize original research and professorial
effort. While the scholarly audience is made up of serious
individual readers, Library of America books are designed to
appeal to a reading public. The handsomely bound volumes have the
appearance of a Bible and are "not so much advertised as announced
... as pieces of a comprehensive patriotic artifact", targeted
more to collectors than to readers.

At the heart of university press animosity towards the
Library of America program is the question of subsidization (an
astounding amount has been given to date by the National Endowment
for the Humanities and the Ford Foundation), aggravated by the
Library's handling of licensing agreements. This leads the
presses--and the author--to question whether the Library is a
private undertaking or a public service. Should the Library's
"noble national ambition of defining and preserving and
disseminating culture" free them of the obligation to pay the
market rate for publishing rights? Finally, the author points out
that university presses are not in a position to "validate some
national notion of the classics" while the Library of America
"presumes not only to approve but to define, with a financial
arrangement that gives that definition power".

Nordloh is professor of English at Indiana University and
former chairman of the Center for Scholarly Editions.

Related reading

"HBJ to Publish 50-volume America's Library by 1985" Publishers
Weekly 215, (April 30, 1979): 22-24.

Kenner, Hugh. "Classics by the Pound." Harper's 265 (August
1982): 73.

III

JOURNAL PUBLISHING

"Facts of Scholarly Publishing" by WILLIAM PELL.
"The Place of the Journal in the Scholarly Communications System"
      by CHARLES OSBURN.
"The Heldref Experience" by CORNELIUS W. VAHLE, JR.
"The Scientist's View of His Information System"
      by J. F. B. ROWLAND
"The Electronic Journal: A Progress Report"
      by MURRAY TUROFF and STARR ROXANNE HILTZ.
"Electronic Publishing: Some Notes on Reader Response and Costs"
      by O. L. STANDERA.
"Requirements for the Scholarly Journal in Transition"
      by ANNE B. PITERNICK.
"Financial Management in Publishing Journals" by MARY E. CURTIS.

Related reading

MLA Directory of Periodicals, 1986-87
      by the Modern Language Association of America.
"Humanities Journals in 1979" by JOHN BUDD.
Publishers and Libraries: A Study of Scholarly and Research
      Journals by BERNARD M. FRY and HERBERT S. WHITE.
"Computer Options for Subscription Fulfillment and Publication
      Management" by DOUGLAS FISHER.
"Why Are New Journals Founded?" by J. F. B. ROWLAND.
"Synopsis Journals as Seen by their Authors" by J. F. B. ROWLAND.
A Study of the Scientific Information System of the United Kingdom
      by The Royal Society.
"The Electronic Journal and its Relatives" by ALAN SINGLETON.
"Electronic Alternatives to Paper-based Publishing in Science and
      Technology" by D. W. KING.
"Electronic and Micrographic Technologies, Cost Effectiveness and
      Accessibility" by IAN MONTAGNES.
"Ways of Viewing Costs of Journals: Cost Evaluation of the BLEND
      Experiment" by ALAN SINGLETON and D. J. PULLINGER.
"The Future of Indexing and Abstracting Services"
      by F. W. LANCASTER and JULIE M. NEWAY.
"Culture and the Media of Communication" by DAN LACY.
"Unconventional Uses of On-line Information Retrieval Systems: On-
      line Bibliometric Studies" by DONALD T. HAWKINS.

PELL, WILLIAM. "Facts of Scholarly Publishing," PMLA (September 1973): 639-70

An excellent introduction to the problems of scholarly publishing, this is the fifth in a series of reports conducted for the Modern Language Association over a period of twenty years. Like the earlier reports, Pell's study reviews the state of journal publishing in the field of language and literature. In addition, it provides a guide to help scholars decide where to submit their articles and a section on book publishing, including a description of the fields of interest for 71 university presses.

Pell surveyed 216 journals to obtain data on circulation, advertising, status and handling of manuscripts, book reviews,and problems for the calendar year 1971. Among his findings on economic issues: increases in cost were outstripping subscription income; average circulation among responding publications was 2,000 to 2,500, but 17 percent of the journals reported a circulation of fewer than 500 copies; journals were highly dependent on library subscriptions; the need for increased subsidies was the biggest worry (most journals reported that subsidies cover 20-30 percent of their operating costs).

On manuscript questions, he found: most journals were using two or three readers to referee each manuscript; the review process was taking about three months; after acceptance the average wait for publication was about a year, with several journals reporting a lag of up to three years; the number of submissions was increasing every year; two out of three journals publish book reviews and review essays; book reviews tended to appear about thirteen months after publication of the book, but the range was three months to three years. (These conditions have changed little since that time.)

On the question of proliferation of journals, editors were divided on the question of whether there were too many or too few journals. Some editors called for more journals to deal with emerging special fields while others deplored the trend toward overspecialization. Many journal editors and press directors blamed the publication requirements for tenure for much of the increase in second rate material on topics of little interest.

Related reading

Modern Language Association of America, MLA Directory of Periodicals, 1986-87. New York: MLA 1986. The biennial listing of journals and serials that are cited in the latest MLA International Bibliography. It includes information on editorial policies, procedures for manuscript submission, advertiser rates, circulation and so on for 3,065 publications. A third of them are published in the United States or Canada; more than a third report a circulation of fewer than 1,000 subscribers. An introductory summary of the data shows that the annual rate of increase in the number of journals in the field has declined since the 1970s.

OSBURN, CHARLES B. "The Place of the Journal in the Scholarly Communications System." Library Resources and Technical Services 28 (October/December 1984): 315-24.

This historical review of journal publication provides an important comparison of current and past uses of journal literature. Osburn observes that the central role of the journal in the creation and transmission of knowledge has changed very little over three hundred years. Beginning with the Journal des Scavans in 1665, these publications have encouraged inquiry and facilitated the flow of information, but where the eighteenth century journal was a medium of education and dissemination of ideas, the nineteenth century publication was aimed at a specialized scientific audience. Rapid publication made journals more appropriate than books for the growing scientific research community, and similar growth patterns subsequently occurred in the humanities and social sciences.

The crucial role of the journal rests on the peer review process, which "remains the essential characteristic of formal scholarly communication." The continuing objectives of the most prestigious journals are to maximize high quality work and uphold the tradition of open and swift information exchange. However, the number of participants in the scholarly communication system has increased and so has the number of journals. Standards of quality are endangered by the sheer weight of numbers. Although the motivations of authors are unlikely to change, new channels for publication are being used as alternatives to journal publishing. In this situation, it is essential to control forces that may diminish the quality of the traditional medium.

Osburn, University Librarian at the University of Cincinnati at the time of this article, is director of libraries at the University of Alabama.

Related reading

Budd, John. "Humanities Journals in 1979." Scholarly Publishing 12 (January 1981): 171-85. The author surveyed 74 humanities journals. A comparison with the results of a 1971 study by William Pell shows a decrease in (a) the number of articles submitted to scholarly journals, (b) the acceptance rate of articles by scholarly journals, and (c) the time needed for evaluation and publication.

Fry, Bernard M., and Herbert S. White. Publishers and Libraries: A Study of Scholarly and Research Journals. Lexington, Mass.: Lexington Books, 1976.

VAHLE, CORNELIUS W., Jr. "The Heldref Experience." Scholarly Publishing 13 (April 1982): 269-79.

The author reviews the history of an innovative experiment in collaboration that enabled a number of independent journals--most of them small and losing money--to survive.

In 1972, the Helen Dwight Reid Educational Foundation (Heldref) became concerned when it learned several excellent journals were in danger of extinction because of financial difficulties. Heldref decided to establish a journal publishing division to keep them going. In the first ten years, it purchased 40 publications, usually by assuming the owner's obligation to fulfill existing subscriptions. The publications were in the fields of education, the humanities, and the social and physical sciences.

Printing costs were reduced by standardizing formats. Typesetting costs were reduced by using in-house composition equipment. Subscriptions were centralized and computerized. These specific changes and other efficiencies achieved by operating at a larger and more efficient scale, enabled Heldref to operate its total program at a break-even point or better even though a number of journals still fail to pay their way. The foundation adheres strictly to a policy of publishing only journals that it owns. Editorial responsibility for each of the journals is vested in a body of three executive editors.

Vahle is director of Heldref Publications.

Related reading

Fisher, Douglas. "Computer Options for Subscription Fulfillment and Publication Management." Paper presented at the annual meeting of the Society for Scholarly Publishing, San Francisco, June 2, 1981.

ROWLAND, J. F. B. "The Scientist's View of his Information System." The Journal of Documentation 38 (March 1982): 38-42.

The Committee on Scientific Information of the Royal Society, London, conducted a three-year survey of scientific information systems. It surveyed biologists, physicists, physical scientists, biochemists, and chemists. Of those solicited, 63 percent responded. By a wide margin the surveyed scientists favored journals printed from camera-ready copy and disapproved electronic journals. They approved of the trend to specialized journals, and a large majority felt there were already enough journals in their field. When asked about their own experiences with on-line retrieval systems, the scientists responded:

> 223 had used them
> 365 had not used them
> 156 of those who had used them were satisfied
> 182 of those who had used them would not again

The survey bore out the idea that traditional attitudes and practices prevail and suggested that most scientists do their own research in journals.

Rowland is a member of the Royal Society, London.

Related reading

Rowland, J. F. B. "Why Are New Journals Founded?" The Journal of Documentation 37 (March 1981): 36-40.

_____. "Synopsis Journals as Seen by their Authors." The Journal of Documentation 37 (June 1981): 69-76.

The Royal Society. A Study of the Scientific Information System of the United Kingdom. London: The Royal Society, 1981. DLRDD Report #5626.

TUROFF, MURRAY and STARR ROXANNE HILTZ. "The Electronic Journal: A Progress Report." Journal of the American Society for Information Science 33 (July 1982): 195-202.

The authors evaluate four journal forms available on the Electronic Information Exchange System (EIES) that are potential replacements for the conventional journal: informal newsletter; unrefereed public conference, or "paper fair"; refereed conventional form, but with electronic variations; and tailored and structured inquiry and response journals. They predict that small computer networks will emerge to replace many journal functions.

The conventional journal is an essential part of the social control system of scholarship. Refereeing, or peer review, is intended to assure publication of the "best" scholarship in a field. Publication, in turn, tends to confer prestige and to increase the resources available for further research. The electronic journal can also serve these functions ideally.

The simplest EIES journal is a newsletter, generally published weekly. It serves as "a current awareness abstract and headline service" for EIES subscribers, allowing access to full-length articles. All past issues are stored online.

EIES has an unrefereed journal aspect called "Paper Fair." Any subscriber can enter a paper and initiate the electronic equivalent of a conference, with readers commenting on or contributing to the original article.

The first electronic journal was an electronic version of the traditional print-based journal. It improves on the conventional journal by allowing articles to be "published" as soon as they are completed and by allowing readers' comments to be published, too.

Tailored "journals" are also possible. An EIES version has three specialized types of text: inquiries, responses, and briefs. Any member of the network may solicit information or responses from other members of the network. When enough responses have been generated, someone prepares a "brief" that integrates the inquiry and the responses.

Turoff and Hiltz are at the New Jersey Institute of Technology, Newark, New Jersey.

Related reading

Singleton, Alan. "The Electronic Journal and its Relatives." Scholarly Publishing 13 (October 1981): 3-18.

King, D. W. "Electronic Alternatives to Paper-based Publishing in Science and Technology." The Future of the Printed Word. Ed. P. J. Hills. London: Frances Pinter, 1980.

STANDERA, O.L. "Electronic Publishing: Some Notes on Reader Response and Costs." Scholarly Publishing 16 (July 1985): 291-305.

The University of Calgary produced an experimental journal on paper, in microfiche, and in "pure" electronic form and compared the three for reader acceptance and cost on the basis of responses from seventy-one faculty members at the University of British Columbia. The study revealed that readers are not enthusiastic about the new medium: only 5 percent of the seventy-one accepted electronic publishing without reservation. At the same time, however, it is becoming easier for authors to submit manuscripts in electronic form.

The Calgary study processed ten papers as an issue of an electronic journal. The "issue" was then presented to twenty readers (ten teachers and ten librarians) in five formats: line-printer copy; letter-quality printer copy; conventional journal; computer-output microfiche; and electronic journal (read on a video-display terminal). The content of all five versions was identical. The readers ranked the journal formats, ranked the relative importance of thirteen factors (such as appearance, timeliness, ease of use), and gave overall comments. The conventional journal scored highest with both groups. Both groups also agreed on the most important criteria: ease of browsing, availability of indexes, and user-friendly procedures. The conventional journal also ranked first in cost-benefit evaluation. Standera concludes that "costs and acceptance ratings must be viewed in the context of changing technology.... The expectation that electronic publishing will mean less cost is unrealistic.... The cost of hardware will continue to decrease while costs of software and human services will grow."

Standera is the technical director of the Electronic Publishing Project in the University Libraries at the University of Calgary.

Related reading

Montagnes, Ian. "Electronic and Micrographic Technologies, Cost Effectiveness and Accessibility." Canadian Journal of Higher Education 13 (1983).

Singleton, Alan, and D. J. Pullinger. "Ways of Viewing Costs of Journals: Cost Evaluation of the BLEND Experiment." Electronic Publishing Review 4 (1984): 59-71.

PITERNICK, ANNE B. "Requirements for the Scholarly Journal in Transition." <u>Scholarly Publishing</u> 14 (October 1982): 49-59.

The journal now exists in various forms: the traditional hard copy; microform; separate articles distributed on demand (photocopy, reprint, abstracting and indexing services); electronic mail; and full text on line. The time is right to exploit the possibilities of new technology. Piternick proposes three rules for publishers who are ready to exploit these possibilities:

1. Journal formats should be appropriate to the medium of communication. Footnotes and appendixes that appear at the end of an article in a hard copy are difficult to find on the microform copy. If an article is disseminated separately, all information pertaining to it should be included with it. Inclusion of all necessary bibliographic information ensures that the article will be properly cited.

2. Bibliographic information should be standardized, not only in the article itself but in citations of it.

3. Subject access should be facilitated. Journals should publish an abstract for each substantive article printed in each issue, and the titles of articles should be as informative as possible. To facilitate the scanning of articles, certain sections--such as introduction, summary, or conclusion--should be designated as high content areas.

Piternick is a professor in the School of Librarianship, University of British Columbia.

Related reading

Lancaster, F. W., and Julie M. Neway. "The Future of Indexing and Abstracting Services." <u>Journal of the American Society for Information Science</u> 33 (September 1982): 183-89.

Lacy, Dan. "Culture and the Media of Communication." <u>Scholarly Publishing</u> 13 (April 1982): 195-210.

Hawkins, Donald T. "Unconventional Uses of On-line Information Retrieval Systems: On-line Bibliometric Studies." <u>Journal of the American Society for Information Science</u> 28 (January 1977): 13-18.

CURTIS, MARY E. "Financial Management in Publishing Journals."
Scholarly Publishing 17 (October 1985): 65-72.

Publishers of journals should measure the performance of
their journals in three ways: as individual journals, as parts of
a journals publication program, and for their responsiveness to
social and technological change.

Each journal should be regarded as a small independent
business and should therefore have a business plan. When starting
up a new journal, the publisher must be clear about how long the
journal can be published before it breaks even and how much of a
return it must produce on that investment. The assumptions that
form the basis for these expectations must be clearly stated.
These assumptions will be adjusted continually as actual results
are compared with the plan. Items to be evaluated include: (1)
actual number of subscriptions and expected revenues, sources and
costs of sales, (2) costs of production (compared against previous
year), other expenses (such as staff expenses), and (3) net
revenues from year to year, before and after expenses.

At the journals program level, publishers must evaluate the
program as a whole as well as the individual journals. A journals
publication program should have "enough concentration in key areas
to permit economies of scale in marketing, but enough diversifi-
cation to keep the program out of trouble if an entire market goes
sour."

Journal publishing costs are only partly the result of
publishing decisions. They are also the result of such larger
social and technological factors as: constrained purchasing
budgets; electronic media; inflation; and rapidly changing market
needs.

This paper is based on an address at a workshop sponsored by
the Association of American Publishers in New York, March 11,
1985.

Curtis, former vice president and publisher of the
periodicals division, John Wiley & Sons, Inc. Publishers, is
senior vice president of Transaction, Inc.

IV

PUBLISHING AND TECHNOLOGY

"The Impact of Technology on Scholarly Publishing"
        by IRVING LOUIS HOROWITZ and MARY E. CURTIS.
"Perspectives on New Technology" by IAN MONTAGNES.
"Editing Joyce's 'Ulysses': An International Effort
        by MICHAEL GRODEN.
"The Collected Works of Erasmus"
        by J. K. McCONICA, and R. M. SCHOEFFEL.
"Computerizing the Oxford English Dictionary" by EDMUND WEINER.

Related reading

Electronic Publishing Plus: Media for a Technological Future
        edited by MARTIN GREENBERGER.
"Computer-Aided Selection of Reviewers and Manuscript Control"
        by LORRIN R. GARSON.
"Authors, Editors, and Computers" by CONSTANCE U. GREASER.
"The Rationale of Copy-Text" by W. W. GREG.
"The Computerized Ulysses" by HUGH KENNER.
"20th Century Technology and the Jefferson Papers"
        by CHARLES T. CULLEN.

HOROWITZ, IRVING LOUIS and MARY E. CURTIS. "The Impact of
Technology on Scholarly Publishing." Scholarly Publishing 13
(April 1982): 211-28.

The authors provide a valuable evaluation of the role of the
publisher in a changing technological environment. Questions
addressed include: (1) how will the new technology affect property
rights and copyright ownership; (2) how will publishers decide
what to print, what to place in archives and what to dispose of;
and (3) what will constitute publication--the production of
material in print alone, or the inclusion of products of the new
technologies. As the definition of what constitutes publishing
becomes more diffuse "marketing and promotion may become the
critical elements distinguishing publication from availability."

The change in the publisher-author relationship is being
shaped in part by the use of word processors which give the author
greater responsibility in the prepublication and dissemination
process. This may lessen the control of the publisher and
increase the author's share of the risks and rewards. One issue
here is whether authors can maintain the publishers' standards.

Scholarly and scientific publishers validate information by
the act of making it public; they serve as "brokers of
innovation", as mediators, as authenticators in facilitating
decisions about promotions and awards. How will these roles
change? Wider acceptance of technology such as online services
may also affect the traditional ways publishers communicate with
their customers; as bibliographic database searching becomes more
routine, investments in direct mail may become less necessary.

As librarians become information managers and research
libraries become information centers on campus, producing
information on demand or alerting researchers to it, those
libraries will assume some of the publisher's functions.
Availability of material then would be associated with a center of
research rather than with a publisher.

Turning to the question of access and who will control it, the
authors write: "We may begin to talk about democracy in terms of
how widely a society permits access to information, to computers,
to photocopying equipment."

Horowitz is Hannah Arendt Distinguished Professor of
Sociology at Rutgers University and President, Transaction, Inc.
Curtis was vice president of John Wiley and Sons before becoming
senior vice president of Transaction.

Related reading

Greenberger, Martin, ed. Electronic Publishing Plus: Media for a
Technological Future. White Plains, New York: Knowledge Industry
Publications, 1985.

MONTAGNES, IAN. "Perspectives on New Technology." <u>Scholarly Publishing</u> 12 (April 1981): 219-29.

Calling the book's invention the first revolution in scholarly communication since the invention of writing, the author briefly traces the history of book production from scriptoria through the invention of movable type and the development of lithography to the growth of university presses. Against this background, he evaluates the role of the computer and calls it "an important tool for scholarship, but not yet directly for scholarly communication," its principal value being as an adjunct to print. He then points out the limitations of the new technology by examining its impact on the functions of publishing:

1. Manuscript appraisal is the most costly process in scholarly publishing and is labor intensive; the impact of technology is minimal.
2. Copy editing is another labor-intensive area but one in which the new technology promises considerable help.
3. In design, which remains almost totally human, beneficial impacts of technology have been minimal.
4. Production is already influenced by the new technology with the union of the computer and phototypesetter. In book and journal production the impact of technology is very high.
5. In marketing, only direct mail is particularly helped by technology. People must still make calls, arrange exhibitions and promotions. Overall, technology's input is moderate.
6. Order fulfillment. Book and subscription orders can be checked on and billed by the computer, but much remains to be done by people. In the warehouse, technology has low impact.
7. In accounting, computers can keep the books but credit control, administration and budgeting remain human functions. Still, the usefulness of technology can be high if the publisher knows how to exploit the computer.

While acknowledging that his survey omits some uses of technology, such as preparing indexes and manipulating bibliographic data, Montagnes emphasizes that the greatest impact of technology is on some production and business functions. Impact is lowest in areas that are at the heart of publishing: appraisal ("the creative decision of what shall be published") and marketing ("the effective distribution of the result").

Montagnes is general editor of the University of Toronto Press and editor of <u>Scholarly Publishing</u>.

Related reading

Garson, Lorrin R. "Computer-Aided Selection of Reviewers and Manuscript Control." <u>Scholarly Publishing</u> 12 (October 1980): 65-74.

Greaser, Constance U. "Authors, Editors, and Computers." <u>Scholarly Publishing</u> 12 (January 1981): 123-30.

GRODEN, MICHAEL. "Editing Joyce's 'Ulysses': An International Effort." Scholarly Publishing 12 (October 1980): 37-54.

A "revised theory of the editing process and an intimate cooperation between human minds and computer technology" have made an international effort to edit Ulysses a major literary event. Just as Thomas Staley, in a 1976 survey of James Joyce studies, was bemoaning the "deplorable condition of the texts of Ulysses and Finnegans Wake" and doubting that definitive editions could be produced soon, Munich editor Hans Walter Gabler was planning the corrected edition of Ulysses which we see today. Writing in 1980, Groden explains the editor's motivation: "No radically new Ulysses lies buried under the compositors' errors, but several thousand richer, more consistent and more comprehensible words and phrases await discovery through editorial effort."

The original edition of Ulysses contained over 8,000 errors-- about one in every thirty words. Joyce was nearly blind and could not proofread carefully; he also added about one-third of the text as he read the proofs. Only one of the French typesetters knew English--just enough to "correct" the author's idiosyncratic language. Since all subsequent versions were full of errors, none could serve as an authoritative edition (copy-text) to which emendations could be made. Thus an alternative to the traditional copy-text basis for editing had to be found. With Joyce's own working methods and manuscripts pointing the way, Gabler recognized that by recreating the author's writing he could arrive at an accurate text. He then modified the idea of copy-text to one of a "continuous manuscript" and shifted the editorial emphasis to one of recovery of this manuscript.

While the continuous manuscript process does not depend on the use of a computer and was developed independently of the editor's decision to use one, Gabler's discovery of a set of four interlocked computer programs (that compare text, print out results, correct and copy) developed for another project at Tubingen and known as "TU-STEP", promised an unprecedented degree of accuracy, completeness, and more: Two versions of edited text--one a synopsis of the textual development and one clear reading text--could be generated, as well as a concordance for Ulysses and eventually for Joyce's entire output.

Groden is associate professor of English at the University of Western Ontario.

Related reading

Greg, W. W. "The Rationale of Copy-Text." Studies in Bibliography 3 (1950-51): 19-36.

Kenner, Hugh. "The Computerized Ulysses." Harper's (April 1980): 89-95.

McCONICA, J. K. and R. M. SCHOEFFEL. "The Collected Works of Erasmus." Scholarly Publishing 10 (July 1979): 313-24.

The University of Toronto Press undertook publication of the Collected Works of Erasmus (CWE) because little was known about this "architect of modern thought." Most of his work has not been translated out of Latin, and it has become less accessible as the number of Latin readers has declined. Erasmus' surviving correspondence comprises more than 3,000 letters. CWE, when completed, will constitute more than sixty volumes, of which twenty-two will be the correspondence. CWE will be as comprehensive as possible for a translation and will use complete texts.

The aim of providing a comprehensive scholarly edition in translation was unprecedented. Among the many problems that have been addressed are standardization of translation and identification of textual change. The volumes of correspondence will be accompanied by a biographical register of the contemporaries Erasmus mentioned in the texts. Separate sub-series dealing with the Adagia and the New Testament scholarship will be accompanied by volumes of critical essays and indexes.

Overall direction of the project has been by an editorial board (eight members), which meets semiannually, with a chairman who applies policy on a day-to-day basis. An executive committee, which also meets semiannually, is the link between editorial activity and publication. Its chairman is responsible for the administrative aspects of publication.

This summary of the originals of the CWE is adapted from the fuller account by R. M. Schoeffel and Prudence Tracy, "In Praise of Folly, or Life in the Underground," Press Notes from the University of Toronto Press (August-October 1979) 12, no. 8-10.

McConica is senior fellow of the Pontifical Institute of Medieval Studies, Toronto, research fellow of All Souls College, Oxford, and chairman of the editorial board of the CWE.

Schoeffel is senior house editor of the University of Toronto Press and chairman of the executive committee of the CWE.

Related reading

Cullen, Charles T. "20th Century Technology and the Jefferson Papers." Scholarly Publishing 13 (October 1981): 45-53.

WEINER, EDMUND. "Computerizing the Oxford English Dictionary."
Scholarly Publishing 16 (April 1985): 239-53.

In May 1984 the Oxford University Press announced its plans
to computerize the Oxford English Dictionary. Weiner describes
the plans for the project: how the original text and supplements
will be integrated electronically, how the present typography and
layout will be preserved, how the database can be designed to meet
users' needs, and how it will be used as an in-house resource.

The first goal in the process is the publication of the New
Oxford English Dictionary in traditional form. That text will be
converted into an electronic database which will be made available
to the public by the early 1990s and will also be used in-house to
keep the OED up to date and as a resource for the lexicographical
staff. A final goal is the expansion of the central database by
the addition of satellite electronic texts, including sound
recordings and video material, which will form a database of the
English language. Linguistic change and the "vital need to ensure
that the Dictionary is a true and complete register of the English
language today" are the key factors in this effort. After the
1933 Supplement to the original Dictionary of 1928 was published,
the staff dispersed leaving no one to monitor the linguistic
changes of the next quarter century. The strength of the new
project lies in its continuity; it overlaps with the previous
phase of Oxford's historical lexicography.

Production of the New OED involves integrating the
Supplements (66,000 entries approximately half of which are main
words) into the main text of the Dictionary--a task that will be
facilitated by electronic technology but requiring development of
a complex computer system. The task involves keyboarding the
text (estimated at 350 million characters); proofreading after
initial entry and again after integration; integration itself
(including checking about 425,000 cross references in the combined
work); designing a system to keep the machine-readable text secure
on the computer, and actual production of the book (63,000 columns
in its present format). The design of the database (by the
University of Waterloo in Canada) is based on user need--
investigated by conducting a survey of professionals in a wide
variety of fields; it will be made public either by mounting (by a
host) for online access or accommodated on an optical digital disk
for exclusive use. Once established, the OED database will be
used for all revisions of the Dictionary and "will almost
certainly turn out to be one of the most valuable tools for
practical lexicography that we could possess."

Weiner is the editor of the New Oxford English Dictionary and
a member of the New OED project team.

V

LIBRARIES: ROLE AND PROSPECTS

The University Library in the United States: Its Origins and
      Development by ARTHUR T. HAMLIN.
Academic Libraries: The Changing Knowledge Centers of Colleges and
      Universities by BARBARA B. MORAN.
Academic Research and Library Resources: Changing Patterns in
      America by CHARLES B. OSBURN.
"Research Libraries and the Dynamics of Change"
      by WARREN J. HAAS.
"The Function and Methods of Libraries in the Diffusion of
      Knowledge" by GORDON R. WILLIAMS.
"Shifting Gears: Information Technology and the Academic Library"
      by RICHARD DE GENNARO.
"The Library: Center of the Restructured University"
      by PATRICIA BATTIN.
Academic Information in the Academic Health Sciences Center: Roles
      for the Library in Information Management
      by NINA W. MATHESON.
"Publishers and Librarians: A Foundation for Dialogue" from
      Library Quarterly.
"Academic Libraries and the Future: A President's View"
      by ROBERT M. O'NEIL.
Books in our Future by the United States Library of Congress.

Related reading

"Research Libraries in the Network Environment"
      by PATRICIA BATTIN.
"Research Libraries Enter the Information Age"
      by RICHARD DE GENNARO.
Libraries, Technology and the Information Marketplace
      by RICHARD DE GENNARO.
"The Academic Library Nexus" by NINA MATHESON.
Priorities for Academic Libraries edited
      by THOMAS J. GALVIN and BEVERLY P. LYNCH."
"The Future of the Book: A Historian's Perspective"
      by EDWARD M. WALTERS.
"Books, Libraries and Scholarly Traditions" by JOHN COLE.

HAMLIN, ARTHUR T. The University Library in the United States:
Its Origins and Development. Philadelphia: University of
Pennsylvania Press, 1981.

Hamlin's monograph is the most comprehensive and
authoritative recent history of university libraries. Beginning
with the colonial period, he devotes the first third of the book
to a chronological narrative of the growth and development of
college and university libraries, the rise of research libraries
between 1876 and 1920, libraries between the wars, and the
expansion of research facilities since World War II. The rest of
the book offers a topical treatment of developments in
librarianship that have been especially important in recent years:
for example, collection building, finances, services, and library
buildings. Special attention is paid to the increase in library
cooperation and the adoption of new technologies. A set of useful
statistical appendices follows the text.

The book is intended for "the academician outside the library
profession who is a user of libraries and interested in them."
The author views the growth of book collections as a major
achievement in American cultural and intellectual history and
emphasizes the importance of library facilities in the
intellectual life of universities and in the society. For those
who wish to follow up this history, ample but not encyclopedic
footnotes provide references to other staples of the library past.
Undoubtedly the most useful current reference is the Journal of
Library History, which reflects a major increase in interest in
this field during the 1970s and 1980s.

Hamlin is director emeritus of libraries, Temple University.

MORAN, BARBARA B. <u>Academic Libraries: The Changing Knowledge Centers of Colleges and Universities</u>. ASHE-ERIC Higher Education Research Report no. 8, 1984. Washington, D.C.: Association for the Study of Higher Education, 1984.

For a useful summary of major issues in the academic library field today, one can hardly do better than consult this study. Written especially for faculty and academic administrators, the report provides a well-balanced discussion of pros, cons, issues, and problems, and deals with topics that have not been much discussed outside the library field. Moran also incorporates much of the current literature on academic librarianship.

The report begins with a section on technology, including the bibliographic utilities, online databases, online public access catalogs, and a section about the electronic library of the present and future. Managerial topics--budgeting, the library director's responsibility to relate the management of library resources to the institutional climate, and the status and role of academic librarians--are the focus of the two next chapters. Questions relating to library collections, and especially the shift from collecting resources to providing access to them, are considered in a final section.

While Moran does not shirk hard questions or minimize the difficulties facing academic libraries, she maintains an optimistic tone. She emphasizes the need for improved planning to meet the new demands of the information revolution. In a concluding series of recommendations, the author encourages faculty and administrators to join in the library planning processes, to provide the necessary financial commitments that will allow libraries to retool, and to support cooperative efforts.

Barbara Moran is assistant professor at the School of Library Science, University of North Carolina.

OSBURN, CHARLES B. <u>Academic Research and Library Resources:</u>
<u>Changing Patterns in America</u>. Westport, Conn.: Greenwood Press,
1979.

Osburn describes the changes that have taken place in
academic research since World War II, and indicates their impact
on research libraries' collection policies, in the context of
diminishing support for higher education and libraries. He
contends that federal funding and federal priorities have changed
the nature of academic research from basic to applied, and cites
other influences, such as the decline in use of foreign research
literature, a shift to more informal communications, and decreased
emphasis on historical precedent. Computer centers and "invisible
colleges" have taken over many functions formerly assigned to
libraries, and current awareness is more highly valued than ever
before. These changes, he believes, have affected the humanities
as well as the social sciences and the sciences, and they have an
important implication for libraries: total collection building is
no longer necessary even in the humanities, since comprehensive
collections seem not to be required to meet modern research
demands.

The crux of the problem is that libraries have not changed
their collection policies so as to better anticipate and meet
researchers' demands. Osburn urges a shift from quantity to
quality in research library collection building, and the use of
national planning and cooperative agreements to strengthen
libraries even as their funding declines. As a goal, he proposes
"full partnership of libraries in a national academic research
system."

Osburn, former university librarian at the University of
Cincinnati, is director of libraries at the University of Alabama.

HAAS, WARREN J. "Research Libraries and the Dynamics of Change," Scholarly Publishing 11 (April 1980): 195-202.

First as a university library director and more recently as president of the Council on Library Resources, Haas has observed firsthand the factors that are shaping research library activities today: rising costs, rapidly increasing collections, the demands of new technologies, and new expectations from users. Their collective influence has forced research libraries to begin a comprehensive review of their operations and relations with each other. Attempts to build new systems quickly while maintaining collections have taxed limited financial resources. Realizing that expanded budgets are unlikely, libraries are looking to technology and cooperative enterprises for assistance. Computers will be used to transmit information important to research library users. This will change the nature of library collecting and services. It also will transform the ways that librarians work, and will influence related enterprises such as publishing.

Two areas basic to the library revolution are bibliographic structure and collection control. Computerized bibliographic databases transcend the individual library's collection by offering access to more publications than any single institution possesses. Individual collections need to be seen as aggregates of discrete parts. Both areas affect and are affected by the ways scholars work. Long established library objectives--effective preservation and use of recorded information, provision of services, and development of appropriate links to scholarly bodies and publishing--will remain paramount. Haas emphasizes that publishers, librarians, and scholars must work together if the scholarly enterprise is to be well served.

Related reading

Battin, Patricia. "Research Libraries in the Network Environment." Journal of Academic Librarianship 6 (May 1980): 68-73. Battin offers an assessment that is similar to that of Warren J. Haas, but places her emphasis on library interdependence and the construction of networks. What is required is a framework for coordinating library cooperation. Since individual libraries can no longer serve all the demands of scholarship, effective cooperative activities at the national level are essential.

De Gennaro, Richard. "Research Libraries Enter the Information Age." Library Journal 104 (November 15, 1979): 2405-10. De Gennaro discusses resource-sharing activities from a historical perspective. He notes that since World War II, libraries have used three different approaches to keep up with the growth in publishing. One is to employ new photographic and electronic technologies to reproduce publications. The second is to develop or enhance mechanisms for sharing collections among libraries. The third combines the first two through the use of computer and communication capabilities that link institutions in networks.

WILLIAMS, GORDON R. "The Function and Methods of Libraries in the Diffusion of Knowledge." Library Quarterly 50 (1980): 58-75.

The theme of this article--access to information--is more discussed in the mid-1980s than at the time it was written, but the emphasis upon the inability of libraries to collect all that is published is an important signal to both scholars and librarians. Williams argues that the role of libraries has changed significantly, but because the change has not been widely understood, there have not been accompanying efforts to revise budget and management priorities. Society is dependent upon libraries for widespread and ready access to recorded information. However, libraries have restricted acquisitions and capital budgets, and cannot afford to collect and preserve all that is published. Since few government or privately endowed research libraries collect in as many fields as university libraries, it has been chiefly the latter that have provided access to the full range of materials needed for scientific, humanistic, and technical education and research.

With limited resources, university libraries cannot continue to grow as they did in the past. Many are acquiring fewer of the new publications than in previous years and adding fewer volumes to their collections as prices increase. The focus on book collections, however, has been merely the means to an end: the collection and preservation of information. In order to fulfill the social need for access to information, librarians must understand that infinite collecting is no longer possible, and that the alternative is to provide users with the ability to obtain material that is not in the library. Administrators should be aware that increases in size are no longer possible, even with such substitutions as microform copies.

It is important to focus attention on the library's purpose rather than its historic means to achieve that purpose. Although new technologies can ease the tasks, they are costly, and it should be remembered that like book collections, technology is only a means to an end. Librarians, funding sources for libraries, and library users need to realize that making publications and information available rather than simply acquired and stored, will require much more interlibrary sharing than in the past. Rather than reducing this necessity, use of new technology seems likely to increase it.

As director of the Center for Research Libraries in Chicago, a "library's library" that obtains, stores and makes available research materials too specialized for local collections, Williams provides a useful perspective on access that has been increasingly accepted in the library world.

DE GENNARO, RICHARD. "Shifting Gears: Information Technology and the Academic Library." Library Journal 109 (June 15, 1984): 1204-09.

The current task of librarians is to manage the transition from collection-centered to access- and service-oriented institutions. The challenge is to continue traditional collections and services while both automating operations such as cataloging and developing the capacity to deal with information in a variety of electronic forms.

These changes will require special funding and managerial innovations to support new methods of fulfilling the library's mission. The new systems are costly, but far more effective than library and information services of the past. Reliance upon consortia and commercial vendors for some services and materials means that additional and more highly skilled staff will be required.

A research library's effectiveness ultimately will be measured by what it can provide rather than what it has. No library can continue to function autonomously in the electronic information age. There are four major tasks:

1. Construct an integrated system with an online catalog and appropriate network interfaces for resource sharing.
2. Convert the card catalog to machine-readable format.
3. Develop local collections continually while obtaining access to scholarly resources elsewhere.
4. Provide for changing space needs during the transition.

De Gennaro states that librarians cannot justify the costs of implementing these objectives on the grounds that expenditures ultimately will be reduced, because they will not. The reasons for making the investment are to provide better support for university research and instructional needs and to maintain the capacity of the library to provide information services in a high technology society. A few universities are wiring their campuses, installing local area networks, and providing faculty and students with microcomputers. Their example will be imitated elsewhere, with pressure coming from faculty, students and librarians. Library funding will be viewed as part of the cost of bringing entire institutions into the information age.

De Gennaro, former director of libraries, University of Pennsylvania, is director of research libraries of the New York Public Library.

Related reading

De Gennaro, Richard. Libraries, Technology and the Information Marketplace. White Plains: Knowledge Industry Publications, 1987. A collection of 33 articles introduced by two new essays--one a retrospective view on the introduction of new technology in the library field, the other a current and forward looking assessment.

BATTIN, PATRICIA.   "The Library: Center of the Restructured
University." College & Research Libraries 45 (May 1984): 170-76.

Battin believes that university traditions have deterred the
type of integrated, long-range planning needed to take advantage
of the revolution in information and communications technologies.
The traditional role of the library was essentially archival and
localized, and organizationally it was isolated from academic
policy councils. But there are now new capacities for accessing
information that do not tie scholars to physical objects in
stationary collections, and different organizational structures
are needed to create and support such enterprises.

Librarians have been creating new communication links among
libraries nationwide to include both print and nonprint materials
in a system for sharing resources. The Council on Library
Resources is funding a large project (the Linked Systems Project)
to develop links to tie large online databases together.

The effectiveness of new systems depends on the university
community's ability to develop a new structure of access to
knowledge. Six major policy areas demand attention from
university officers and coordination of disparate elements of the
university community:

1. Centralized financial and technological planning to
accommodate archival obligations, introduction of high
technology, large capital costs, integration of services, and
provision of access to external databases;
2. Integration of information services with academic
programs and priorities;
3. Improving access to scholarly resources;
4. Development of electronic publishing;
5. Implications of copyright and ownership questions;
6. Research and development in information technology.

Battin believes that the most important issue is the need for
a cooperative, unified voice for all scholarly endeavors, since
new technologies will require an unprecedented cooperative effort.
Modern technology has essentially superseded the university
structure of a collection of autonomous units. Survival of the
library function as central to research and education is
essential; it is the only unit that contains the understanding of
overall scholarly communication. Elements of the new capacities
are contained in the traditional library organization. Rather
than jettison a tradition of scholarly support because of some
library shortcomings, existing talents and expertise should be
drawn into the institutional effort to re-invent the university
for the electronic age.

Battin, former vice president and university librarian at
Columbia University, is president of the Commission on
Preservation and Access.

MATHESON, NINA.   Academic Information in the Academic Health
Sciences Center: Roles for the Library in Information Management.
Washington, D.C.: Association of American Medical Colleges, 1982.
Reprinted as the October issue of the Journal of Medical Education
(v. 57, no. 2, pt. 2).

Matheson, formerly of the Planning Office, National Library
of Medicine, prepared this report for the Association of American
Medical Colleges. Although the title indicates applicability to a
specific set of libraries, the report has been widely recognized
in the library community as a paradigm for libraries as they enter
the new field of information management. The author considers the
literature in the field and draws upon site visits and a 1980
Delphi study of directors of health sciences libraries to describe
the implications of changing information technologies and the ways
in which libraries can exploit new technologies successfully.

The author begins with the premise that too little attention
has been devoted to upgrading academic information systems and
that the academic community is generally unaware of its dependence
upon those systems. Although it is tempting in times of financial
stringency to reduce these resources, Matheson argues that
improvements in institutional capabilities cannot wait since more
and more information is available only in computer-based systems.
A network system that accommodates collegial relationships and
allows building personal information files from institutional
resources is most effective. There are two options: to create a
new facility or to adapt an existing unit to develop and manage
information resources. Adaptation will occur in stages; the
essential first step is to transform the library "from a
repository to an interactive information transfer and management
system" linking every part of a medical center, and tying centers
to other medical centers and external information sources.

For the biomedical community, the National Library of
Medicine is the logical network coordinator on the national level.
It will need substantial assistance from academic health science
centers, professional associations and societies, and public and
private agencies. The author recommends that health sciences
centers and hospitals begin by upgrading technology and
implementing networks within their institutions. Government
agencies and private business are asked to recognize their
responsibilities to support development of prototype networks,
technology integration programs, and recruiting programs for
professionals needed to develop systems.

Matheson is librarian of the Welch Medical Library, the Johns
Hopkins University.

Related reading

Matheson, Nina. "The Academic Library Nexus." College & Research
Libraries 45 (May 1984): 207-13.

69

Publishers and Librarians: A Foundation for Dialogue.
Proceedings of the Forty-Second Conference of the Graduate Library
School, May 13-15, 1983, Library Quarterly 54 (January 1984).

These proceedings present the results of an effort to bring
publishers and librarians together to discuss common problems from
their different perspectives.

Several of the principals debated the place of technology in
publishing and libraries, and described the problems introduced by
the facilitation of copying and resource sharing by libraries, and
the proliferation of publications and the relinquishment of
quality control functions by publishers. Frederick A. Praeger,
Westview Press, discussed the traditional symbiotic relationship
between publishers, librarians, and scholars and the ways in which
technological innovation has allowed each party to bypass the
others. He cited a renewed consciousness of interdependence as
the base for dealing constructively with the challenge. Yet
although the future of technology and its role as an irresistible
force was a matter for controversy, and considerable debate (as in
the papers presented by Praeger and Peter Urbach, of Pergamon
International Information Corporation), both publishers and librarians expected to exploit it to increase efficiency and possibly
gain relief from costs.

Other tensions arise between seemingly opposing forces within
each sector: for publishers, commercial success versus obligation
to produce creative literature and enduring cultural material; for
librarians, the urge to build collections against the need to
provide services, and the mandate to preserve the culture but also
win popular support. Jay Lucker, library director at MIT,
emphasized that it is the availability of funds, rather than
photocopying, resource sharing, or other techniques to enhance
library resources, that is the determinant of libraries'
acquisitions programs, and Charles Osburn, university librarian,
the University of Cincinnati, discussed the place of collection
development, concentrating upon the concept of selectivity, and
ending with suggestions for broadening collaboration between
publishers and librarians.

Lester Asheim, University of North Carolina, noted shared
stresses and motivations, while recognizing that commercial and
economic forces affect the two communities differently and that
both are to some extent insensible or careless of the long-range
damage caused to the other. His conclusion that publishers and
librarians need to come to terms with new technology and retain
the best in publishing and library tradition in the context of
mutual service to society was meant as a foundation for continuing
dialogue.

O'NEIL ROBERT M.   "Academic Libraries and the Future: A
President's View." College & Research Libraries 45 (May 1984):
184- 88.

O'Neil hypothesizes an opportunity to redesign the standards
and process by which libraries are judged, and provides his own
criteria: interinstitutional cooperation for complementary
collection development; acceptance of new technologies and in a
related sense, institutional adaptation to new methods of
information storage and production; preservation of library
resources; a clear appraisal of the role of the library in the
total educational process; and the roles of libraries and their
users in university governance. Finally, he emphasizes that the
library is central to the university commitment to intellectual
freedom.

In order to implement these criteria, the author suggests
deemphasizing quantitative measures of library status, since they
too frequently are taken to represent quality and encourage
competition rather than encouraging cooperative collection
development and preservation. Rather, it might be possible
through the accreditation process to give more attention to the
more difficult to measure factors such as governance,
bibliographic instruction, professional service, and protection of
intellectual freedom.

At the time of writing, O'Neil was president of the
University of Wisconsin System. He is now president of the
University of Virginia.

Related reading

Galvin, Thomas J. and Beverly P. Lynch eds. Priorities for
Academic Libraries. New Directions for Higher Education #39,
September 1982. San Francisco: Jossey-Bass, 1982. This
collection provides a briefing for administrators on the role of
the library as a central component of the academic enterprise.
The authors have marshalled an impressive array of authors, most
of them librarians, to explain the "splendid complexity" of
university libraries: Robert M. O'Neil on the university administrator's perspective, William Moffatt on the librarian's
perspective, Russell Shank on users' needs, Richard Talbot on
finances, Charles Osburn on collection development, Ward Shaw on
resource sharing, Patricia Battin on preservation, Millicent D.
Abell and Jacquelyn Coolman on staffing, and Robert Plane on the
future.

U.S. Library of Congress. <u>Books in Our Future</u>. Washington, D.C.:
Government Printing Office, 1984.

In 1983 Librarian of Congress Daniel Boorstin obtained
congressional authorization for a study of future changes in the
role of the book. An Advisory Committee on the Book in the
Future, which included educators, librarians, publishers,
scientists, and others, gathered information from a broad spectrum
of individuals and held discussions on the issues, after which
Boorstin prepared this report. Noting that some of the
consultants did not agree with the conclusions, he states that a
supplementary volume including all advisors' views would be
issued. The report is limited in scope and in its treatment of
issues, but it contains an eloquent statement of the importance of
books to society. It touches on important issues such as
illiteracy, aliteracy, and the interaction of the book and new
technologies. The Librarian is optimistic about the prospect that
technologies can be combined for the advancement of an infinitely
adaptable book. To rally the public to fight the problems of
illiteracy, he provides a long list of projects in progress and
proposed. He concludes with a list of recommendations for
Congress, the Executive Branch, and LC itself. Together with the
program of the Library's Center for the Book, which exists to
promote books and reading, this summary report and the study that
led to it illustrate an effort by the nation's largest library to
provide leadership on broad policy issues related to literacy and
access to information and knowledge.

Related reading

Walters, Edward M. "The Future of the Book: A Historian's
Perspective." <u>Information Technology and Libraries</u> 1 (March 1982):
15-21. Walters, director of libraries at the University of Texas,
Dallas, believes that there will be both continuity and change,
and that libraries will have to deal with both old and new forms
of text storage, with books and electronic media. However, he
proceeds from the assumption that the issue of primary concern is
change in research methods and incorporation of technology into
the research process. Distinguishing between cumulative
(scientific) knowledge and noncumulative (social science and
humanities) research, he notes that there are differences in the
ways these groups of disciplines use the scholarly communication
system, and contends that research also may require different
formats depending on whether the subject is approached as basic or
applied research.

Cole, John. "Books, Libraries, and Scholarly Traditions."
<u>Scholarly Publishing</u> 13 (October 1981): 31-43. Librarians and
scholars are now forced by economic constraints to cooperate in
resource sharing schemes, but without many precedents for such
cooperation. Most of the progress in this area has occurred
through work funded by foundations which have brought scholars,
librarians, and university administrators together to discuss
research library needs. Another "bridge-builder" is the Center
for the Book in the Library of Congress. As director of the
Center, Cole provides a brief review of its role.

VI

LIBRARIES AND COMPUTING

"Computing in Documentation and Scholarly Research"
      by WARREN J. HAAS.
"Scholarly Information" by WILLIAM Y. ARMS.
"Academic Libraries and Computing: A Time of Change"
      by C. LEE JONES.
"Building Networks for Scholarly Information"
      by RICHARD McCOY and WAYNE E. DAVISON.
Beyond Bibliography by FREDERICK KILGOUR.
"Science, Scholarship and the Communication of Knowledge"
      by F. W. LANCASTER and LINDA C. SMITH.
Libraries and Librarians in an Age of Electronics
      by F. W. LANCASTER.
"Electronic Publishing, Libraries and the Survival of Information"
      by GORDON B. NEAVILL.
Books, Libraries, and Electronics by E. J. SIGEL, et al.
"Merging Libraries and Computer Centers: Manifest Destiny or
      Manifestly Deranged?" by RAYMOND K. NEFF.

Related reading

"How Significant is Computing for Higher Education?"
      by RICHARD L. VAN HORN.
Campus of the Future: Conference on Information Resources
      by Online Computer Library Center.
Libraries and Information Science in the Electronic Age
      edited by HENDRIK EDELMAN.
"The Electronic Library: A Vision for the Future"
      by PATRICIA BATTIN.
"Local Area Networking Project: Colorado's IRVING Project"
      by FRAN HOOKER.
Library Networks, 1986-87: Libraries in Partnership
      by SUSAN K. MARTIN.
"EIDOS: Beyond Bibliographies" by ROBERT M. MASON.
Toward Paperless Information Systems by F. W. LANCASTER.
"The Paperless Society Revisited" by F. W. LANCASTER.
The End of Libraries by JAMES THOMPSON.
"The Paperless Society" from International Forum for Information
      and Documentation.
"Electronic Publishing and its Impact on Libraries: A Literature
      Review" by MEREDITH BUTLER.
"On Paperless-ness" by NEIL A. CAMPBELL.
"Some Possible Future Effects of Information Technology"
      by MAURICE B. LINE.
The Future of the Printed Word edited by PHILIP HILLS.
Trends in Information Transfer edited by PHILIP HILLS.
Multi-Media Communications by MAY KATZEN.

HAAS, WARREN J. "Computing in Documentation and Scholarly Research." Science 215 (1982): 857-61.

Haas discusses the changes in scholarly communication that technology is bringing about and the organizational and economic issues that must be resolved if the new capabilities are to be employed wisely. The uncontrolled growth of published literature, especially journals, has frustrated producers and users alike, and has aroused concerns among administrators. Transformation of the system by application of computer technologies is essential for maintaining publishing capabilities and controlling expenditures.

Computers also have influenced cataloging and indexing procedures and especially, the dissemination of bibliographic information. With the development of computerized library service systems such as the Online Computer Library Center (OCLC) and the Research Libraries Group (RLG), it has become possible to support several library applications, including online catalogs, interlibrary loans, and acquisitions. Long-term programs in cooperative collection development and preservation also are helping member research libraries address some of the difficulties facing the scholarly communication process. In the long term, these large bibliographic systems need to be linked together to reduce redundant efforts. The Library of Congress and the major bibliographic systems are undertaking this work.

Computers have not had much effect on the actual provision of library materials. Delivery is still governed largely by the format in which an item is stored. Loans and the making of copies are subject to institutional and legal constraints. Questions of demand, costs, funding, and legality must be settled before systems for storage, delivery and use can be mounted. Other important issues not yet resolved include the public-private sector relationship, and the manner in which information created with public funds will be distributed; constraints on the international flow of computerized bibliographic information; and copyright restrictions and protecting the rights of authors.

The new computerized services complement rather than replace existing services, and the high capital and continuing investments imply new pricing structures for information. The special irony of these costs, Haas notes, is that universities produce much of the scholarly record, yet they must buy back what they provided at prices that endanger the capacity to continue at previous levels. While the scholarly world cannot determine the future technology of information services, it has an obligation to make sure that its institutions and organizations are not jeopardized by the competition for funding and the high costs of new systems.

Haas is president of the Council on Library Resources.

ARMS, WILLIAM Y. "Scholarly Information." EDUCOM Bulletin 18
(Fall-Winter 1983):21-23.

Researchers begin their work by assembling information from
many sources, local and worldwide. Computing can improve the data
gathering process but its successful application requires
coordination. The areas from which information comes, within even
a single institution, are likely to be many and varied.

Libraries provide access to books and information services,
and today have large machine-readable databases of shared
cataloging records. Secondary information services available
through libraries include online bibliographic searching of
indexes and specialized bibliographic databases. Extensions of
library computing have involved maps and manuscripts, and other
university collections such as artifacts, paintings, films, and
photographs sometimes are included. Progress for nonbook
materials, however, has been slower. Several universities have
centers for collecting data archives, and some academic
disciplines use databases from the commercial sector such as news
services. University computing systems have generally developed in
isolation from the other information services.

Each service has different visions for integration.
Librarians are interested in integrating services to scholars,
internal data processing, and links to other libraries. Scholars,
however, would like to be able to link information services to
their own personal files or computers. In the future, only the
university will be able to coordinate all the services of
suppliers of information, both on and off campus. Key factors in
the computerized system are quality control, standardization of
equipment, campus communication networks, a homogeneous user
interface, and long-term planning for adoption of new technology
and access to new sources of information. Arms ends by emphasizing the importance of integrating services via standardization and
by cautioning that adequate flexibility must be retained.

The author was vice provost for computing and planning,
Dartmouth college at the time of the article. He is now in charge
of computing at Carnegie-Mellon University.

Related reading

Van Horn, Richard L. "How Significant is Computing for Higher
Education?" EDUCOM Bulletin 20 (Spring 1985): 6-8. As former
provost of Carnegie-Mellon University, and currently chancellor of
the University of Houston-University Park, Van Horn has been
involved with large-scale institutional systems development. His
topic is the strategy of resource development, a subject that he
believes has been neglected because universities have been so
absorbed in the technical aspects of computing. He favors a broad
systems approach as the best means of determining how to use
computing to improve education.

JONES, C. LEE. "Academic Libraries and Computing: A Time of
Change." EDUCOM Bulletin 20 (Spring 1985): 9-12.

As consultant to the Council on Library Resources, Jones has
worked since 1978 with the Bibliographic Service Development
Program, which has been much concerned with the application of new
technology to research library bibliographic processes. This
article provides an overview of developments from a national
perspective. Jones first describes the current (1985) situation:
libraries are using computers to perform traditional tasks such as
producing catalog cards, and some are moving into new
applications, for example, online catalogs. However, progress is
uneven across the population of libraries, and there is no
indication yet of change in the fundamental style of operation.
Recent progress in the area of artificial intelligence and expert
systems, machine publishing, and disk storage formats shows what
may lie ahead in the near term. But it is increasingly evident
that libraries and computer centers deal with the same service:
the delivery of information to the academic community. An
integrated approach to this task needs to be developed. In the
future it is probable that both will be nodes in a complex network
accessed by individual users in different ways, even though users
are, like libraries, at different stages in their acceptance of
computerization.

To prepare for this future, the library community must review
the appropriateness of the bibliographic record structure and
devise a system of obtaining bibliographic data through the
publishing process. Linking systems and implementing electronic
manuscript codes are important tasks for the library and computing
communities, and computer centers need to pay attention to data
security questions. Inter-organizational rivalries still
constrain progress in the library community, and library-publisher
tensions have not been dispelled. Computer centers should direct
attention to the difficulties caused by the existence of many
networks. In the legislative arena, thought needs to be given to
telecommunications cost relief and copyright legislation that
incorporates the new technologies. The future will not be limited
to traditional library services, but will focus on delivery of
needed information whenever and wherever it is required.

Related reading

Online Computer Library Center. Campus of the Future: Conference
on Information Resources. Dublin, Ohio: OCLC, 1987.

Edelman, Hendrik, ed. Libraries and Information Science in the
Electronic Age, Philadelphia: ISI Press, 1986.

Battin, Patricia. "The Electronic Library: A Vision for the
Future." EDUCOM Bulletin 19 (Summer 1984).

McCOY, RICHARD and WAYNE E. DAVISON. "Building Networks for
Scholarly Information." EDUCOM Bulletin 20 (Spring 1985): 2-5, 8.

The authors describe new computer capabilities that will link
library collections and trace the implications for scholarship.
Scholars' views of research libraries are likely to change
considerably in the future: they will think of libraries less
often as places and more frequently as gateways to information
obtained through computer systems. Access to local, regional,
national and international resources will be facilitated by such
efforts as the Linked Systems Project (LSP), in which several
organizations are building the technical means of tying together
their large databases of library catalog records and other
library-related information. Sponsored by the Council on Library
Resources, the LSP employs a specific set of communication
procedures, but leaves each institution free to decide how best to
implement the man-machine interface.

The LSP is implementing two capabilities: the retrieval of
catalog records and the transfer of the bibliographic information
from the source to a local data base. Members of the Linked
Systems Project are the Library of Congress, Washington Library
Network (now the Western Library Network), and the Research
Libraries Group. The Online Computer Library Center (OCLC) joined
in 1985, and links to vendors and other major libraries are
planned. The authors describe the use of the RLG database and the
system links to share collection information, for individual
searching, for retrieving visual images stored on videodisk, and
to access non-Roman language materials.

McCoy was president and Davison was assistant director of
research and development of the Research Libraries Group, Inc.
(RLG), a consortium of large universities and research
institutions.

Related reading

Hooker, Fran. "Local Area Networking Project: Colorado's IRVING
Project," Wilson Library Bulletin 60 (September 1985): 38-42.
The description of this project—which has the potential for
linking every library in the state—is a useful reminder that
academic and research libraries have no monopoly on innovation.
It also indicates that any national system will include more than
research library resources; public libraries are working to become
part of that system.

Martin, Susan K. Library Networks, 1986-87: Libraries in
Partnership. White Plains: Knowledge Industry Publications, 1986.
This is a successor to the first edition issued in 1976.

KILGOUR, FREDERICK. <u>Beyond Bibliography</u>, the Third British
Library Annual Research Lecture, 1984. London: The British
Library Board, 1985.

The Founder Trustee of Online Computer Library Center (OCLC),
Frederick Kilgour, calls on libraries to play a more active role
in the design, development, and use of computer technology for
bibliographic and general research purposes. He believes
libraries should move beyond merely collecting information to
evaluating and disseminating that information to the public.

He sees the new role for libraries emerging from the
development of fifth generation computers, commonly referred to as
knowledge information processing systems, or KIPS. In addition to
the logical problem-solving capabilities of present day computers,
KIPS will be able to infer, associate, and "intuit" information
and communicate it in the user's own language, be that everyday
speech, graphics, musical notations or mathematical symbols. KIPS
are expected to be in use by the 1990s.

Kilgour finds the standard, traditional library a "passive"
and "monolithic arrangement of volumes and catalog entries" that
does not distinguish between, and thus fails to respond to, the
needs of users. Studies have shown that most libraries fail up to
60 percent of the time to provide the information requested by
their users. Kilgour argues that such a lamentable state of
affairs can be corrected with the aid of a system such as KIPS,
with its unique search features and access to both published and
unpublished materials. Kilgour envisions a future "active
library" in which users, with computer guidance, become their "own
reference librarians".

The author sees the beginning of such a library in the
Electronic Information Delivery Online System (EIDOS), now in a
developmental stage at OCLC. EIDOS will permit the user to
retrieve online from a central data base any relevant page or
section of a text, without retrieving the entire text online, or
without gaining possesion of the physical text itself.

The author cites insufficient knowledge about users as the
principal obstacle to development of online services such as
EIDOS, and he closes his lecture by listing four questions
requiring further research: (1) What is the end-use of information
and who are the end-users? (2) What is the information that is
consulted or used most intensively in books? (3) How many texts
are required for a valid field test? and (4) How can knowledge-
based systems improve user access to online information?

Related reading

MASON, ROBERT M. "EIDOS: Beyond Bibliographies," <u>Library Journal</u>,
111 (November 1, 1986): 46-47. A clear, concise overview of
EIDOS, focussing on both the mechanics of the system as well as
its practical application and benefits.

LANCASTER, F.W., and LINDA C. SMITH, "Science, Scholarship and the Communication of Knowledge." Library Trends 26 (Winter 1978): 367-68.

Lancaster and Smith provide a comprehensive discussion of formal and informal communication channels and how they change over time. The advent of the computer and of machine-readable databases is introduced as the factor that has altered secondary publications in the scientific communication system--abstracting and indexing services, printed handbooks and data tables, and directories--and that may in time transform primary publication formats.

Special library services, the authors note, do not differ substantially in kind today from those of earlier years, but librarians have become more active participants on teams of science researchers. National libraries and information analysis centers provide the major automated secondary reference sources, and government funding has allowed the production and dissemination of research in microfiche and via online systems. Communications technology, in the National Institutes of Health Information Exchange Groups extending to even the "invisible colleges," has drawn the scientific community together through computer conferencing and electronic mail service. However, physical access to publications has by no means kept pace with access to colleagues and information about publications.

Scientists report looking not for more information but for more effective ways of obtaining and processing it via use of selectivity, evaluation, review, and synthesis. Secondary literature is growing at about the same rate as primary literature, and the growing scatter increases the difficulty for both scientists and librarians of keeping up, and especially of addressing the growing number of interdisciplinary research problems. Simultaneously, improved awareness of ongoing research has resulted in a preference for informal channels as the only fast means of obtaining information on current projects, and decreased interest in formal library and information center channels.

Lancaster and Smith believe that the improvements made by online systems will be applied to larger and larger bodies of literature. In the end, it is likely that print publications will be replaced with electronic systems. In their view, the current system is a transitional one, and can be expected to evolve toward electronic data banks, beginning with secondary publications, journals, and reference books.

The authors are faculty members at the University of Illinois, Urbana-Champaign.

LANCASTER, F. W. Libraries and Librarians in an Age of
Electronics. Arlington, Va.: Information Resources Press, 1982.

In this book, Lancaster brings together his writings on
evolving technology, the paperless society, and the implications
of the technological revolution for libraries. His purpose is to
stimulate librarians to reassess the library's role. Such
reassessment is absolutely essential, since he believes that
"electronic communications will largely replace print-on-paper
publishing, and that libraries as we know them will become
obsolete." Drawing on writers such as Peter Drucker and Alvin
Toffler, Lancaster presents a forecast of what social changes may
occur in the next two decades, and then reviews the technological
developments that will affect libraries. The evidence for his
predictions includes Delphi studies, vendor plans for new
products, and cost projections, with "future scenarios"
extrapolated from the data. The conclusions do not always appear
to follow from the data, and at times it is difficult to
discriminate between current practice, future probabilities, and
future possibilities. The author's assumption that there is a
contest for supremacy between print and electronics has been
challenged by other experts (see the entry that follows by Sigel
and others.)

Lancaster views the library of the future as a node in
paperless systems, providing access to and expert assistance in
the use of online resources, collecting local interest materials,
integrating electronic systems with materials remaining in print
format, and constructing high quality selection, indexing, and
dissemination systems. Since a librarian's work can no longer be
defined by traditional library processes, he points out that
future education for librarianship should emphasize machine-
readable resources and methods of exploiting them.

Related reading

Lancaster, F.W. Toward Paperless Information Systems. 1978. The
first important exposition of Lancaster's belief that paper would
be replaced by electronics.

Lancaster, F.W. "The Paperless Society Revisited." American
Libraries 16 (September 1985): 553-55. In this later article,
Lancaster makes it clear that he has not changed his views.

Thompson, James. The End of Libraries. London: Bingley, 1982.

"The Paperless Society." International Forum for Information and
Documentation 7 (October 1982). Entire issue.

Butler, Meredith. "Electronic Publishing and its Impact on
Libraries: A Literature Review." Library Resources and Technical
Services 28 (January/March 1984): 41-57.

NEAVILL, GORDON B. "Electronic Publishing, Libraries, and the Survival of Information." Library Resources and Technical Services 28 (January/March 1984): 76-89.

Scholars and librarians, long tied to books, need to consider what new problems may confront researchers in a paperless society. Neavill is especially concerned about the survival of the accumulated store of learning. Unlike printed materials, electronically recorded information can be easily altered and quickly discarded. The corollary of this malleability is transience; there is no assurance that information in an electronic system will survive. Libraries have traditionally assumed the role of keeping the stock of recorded knowledge, but concern with the social role of the library--that is, the distribution and use of information--may lead to neglect of the archival function. Commercial vendors of databases and information systems are not likely to be concerned with the retention of the information they include. Several categories of information are likely to be endangered: scholarly contributions for which there is little or no demand; nonscholarly writings that have served the purpose for which they were created; and works in which information is changed. If retention cannot be justified in economic terms, much material may simply be purged.

It is very important, Nevill argues, to make sure of archival file retention, since reopening old channels of inquiry sometimes leads to important results, and because historians and sociologists are unable to do their work without the historical record. Special attention also needs to be given the protection and care of computer memory, or a disaster may destroy part of society's accumulated wisdom.

Publishing in an electronic environment will raise new implications since a work can be disseminated, updated, or revised, as a whole or in part, at any time. Bibliographical control of different versions of a publication will be difficult, and citations to documents will be of questionable value. These difficulties can be compared with the disadvantages of traditional scientific journal publication as enumerated by Lancaster and discussed by Campbell and others cited below.

Neavill is on the faculty of the Graduate School of Library Science, University of Alabama.

Related reading

Campbell, Neil A. "On Paperless-ness." Canadian Library Journal 41 (August 1984): 181-86.

Line, Maurice B. "Some Possible Future Effects of Information Technology." IFLA Journal 10 (1984): 57-62.

SIGEL, E., et. al. <u>Books, Libraries, and Electronics</u>. White Plains, N.Y.: Knowledge Industry Publications, Inc., 1982.

While Lancaster envisages a transformation in our approach to information, others caution that applications are seldom as fast and far-reaching as they are predicted to be. Those who see the future as a mix of old and new are represented in three British collections (cited below), and this American counterpart, which is also the most recent of the four, appears most useful to U.S. scholars. It includes attention to practical applications of new technologies in publishing and libraries, and the authors also present their speculations on what the future may bring. Although the issues are well drawn, the conclusions are, predictably, inconclusive because development has been too rapid to allow for much more than educated guesses. Yet the message is clear: new library practices are likely to evolve as the result of new technologies, but not necessarily due to conflict between print and electronics.

Sigel is executive vice president and editor-in-chief, Knowledge Inudustry Publications.

Related reading

Hills, Philip, ed. <u>The Future of the Printed Word</u>. Westport, Conn.: Greenwood Press, 1980.

Hills, Philip, ed. <u>Trends in Information Transfer</u>. Westport, Conn.: Greenwood Press, 1982.

Katzen, May. <u>Multi-Media Communications</u>. Westport Conn.: Greenwood Press, 1982.

NEFF, RAYMOND K. "Merging Libraries and Computer Centers:
Manifest Destiny or Manifestly Deranged?" EDUCOM Bulletin 20
(Winter 1985): 8-12.

Neff observes that the idea of merging the library and the
computer center arises from similarities between the two that
become more marked as libraries automate their functions. Eight
trends could lead either to mergers or more sharing of
responsibilities:

1. Computerized libraries provide a new service: the
manipulation of information;
2. Libraries provide access to computer databases and help
users customize the output;
3. The "library model" of providing free access will soon
spread to the computer center;
4. Access to information is more and more open to individual
users through computer networks;
5. Information sharing will increase as intercampus networks
are formed;
6. Libraries and computer centers will have the same kinds
of archival storage devices and union catalogs of data and
software will exist;
7. Information will increasingly be stored in standard
machine-readable format, and will be transmitted and retrieved as
desired;
8. It will be possible to search the library electronically.

Noting that institutions now are building workstations and
networks to bring computing to individual users, Neff describes
the capabilities that this will provide for students and faculty.
Conversion projects to make data machine-readable and technologies
that will ease this task are also discussed. The University of
California-Berkeley has developed a comprehensive strategy which
specifies one campus communications network, a computing
hierarchy, and all-purpose workstations. The library will serve
as the academic information system while the computer center
provides the back-up and archiving service. In conclusion, he
provides some thoughts on establishing rational computer policies
in higher education.

Neff is assistant vice chancellor of information systems and
technology at the University of California-Berkeley.

VII

ONLINE SERVICES

"Online Searching and Computer Programming: Some Behavioral
    Similarities" by CHARLES T. MEADOW.
"Electronic Databases" by MARTHA E. WILLIAMS.
"Information Search Tactics" by MARCIA J. BATES.
Financing Online Search Services in Publicly Supported Libraries
    by MARY JO LYNCH.
"Large Databases, Small Computers and Fast Modems...An Attorney
    Looks at the Legal Ramifications of Downloading"
    by THOMAS S. WARRICK.

Related reading

"Where Do we Go from Here?" by PAULINE ATHERTON COCHRANE.
"Is There a Future for the End User in Online Bibliographic
    Searching?" by SYLVIA G. FAIBISOFF and JITKA HURYCH.
"Experiences in Training End-User Searchers" by JUDITH S. HAINES.
"BRS/After Dark: The Birth of Online Self-Service"
    by RICHARD V. JANKE.
"Online After Six: End User-Searching Comes of Age"
    by RICHARD V. JANKE.
"On-Line Systems: History, Technology, and Economics"
    by CHARLES P. BOURNE.
"On-Line Information Retrieval Bibliography, 1964-1979"
    by DONALD T. HAWKINS.
"Online Reference Service: How to Begin--A Selected Bibliography"
    by EMELIE J. SHRODER.
"Full-Text Databases" by CAROL TENOPIR
"Nonbibliographic On-Line Data Base Services"
    by JUDITH WANGER and RUTH N. LANDAU.
"Search Techniques" by MARCIA J. BATES.
"The Process of Searching Online Bibliographic Databases: A Review
    of Research" by CAROL HANSEN FENICHEL.
"Online Bibliographic Search Strategy Development"
    by DONALD T. HAWKINS and ROBERT WAGERS.
"The Reference Interview in the Computer-Based Setting"
    by SARAH KNAPP.
"Pricing of Online Services for Nonprimary Clientele"
    by RICHARD J. BEELER and ANTOINETTE L. LUECK
"A Cost Accounting Model for Online Computerized Literature
    Searching" by BERT R. BOYCE.
"Fee-for-Information: Legal, Social, and Economic Implications"
    by LESLEY BUHMAN.
"Financial Management of Online Services: A How to Guide"
    by HELEN DRINAN.
"To Charge or Not to Charge: A Rationale" by JOHN LINFORD.
"Using a Microcomputer to Communicate: Part 1: The Basics"
    by CAROL HANSEN FENICHEL.

"Problems and Challenges of Downloading for Database Producers"
     by ARNOLD A. JANSEN.
"Copyright Protection for Bibliographic, Numeric, Factual, and
     Textual Databases" by JEROME K. MILLER.
"Downloading Overview" by LARRY N. OSBORNE.
"Online Searching with a Microcomputer: Downloading Issues"
     by CAROL TENOPIR.

MEADOW, CHARLES T. "Online Searching and Computer Programming: Some Behavioral Similarities (Or Why End Users Will Eventually Take Over the Terminal)." Online 3 (January 1979): 49-52.

This early article on a now recognized issue challenges intermediaries to cast aside their assumption that only professional searchers can do online searching. The author makes a convincing argument for an increase in end-user searching in the near future. From his early background in mathematics and computer programming, Meadow draws an analogy between programming and online searching. Just as programming languages develop to become easier to use and to allow various levels of programming expertise, so will online command languages develop. There will be a role for the end-user searcher as well as for the "highly skilled professional" who will handle the "top of the line" searches. The reference interview process will become more important. It will require the intermediary to assess the online knowledge of the requestor in addition to analyzing the topic to be searched. More online searching will be conducted at all levels with the online intermediary operating on a higher professional level.

Written before the creation of the new online systems and software that are targeted to an end-user market, this article anticipated many of the developments of online searching in the 1980s. It is valid today not only as an historical piece, but because it intuitively describes the search process and end-user motivation for searching.

Meadow, professor of information science at Drexel University when he wrote the article, is now at the University of Toronto, Graduate School of Library and Information Science.

Related reading

Cochrane, Pauline Atherton. "Where Do We Go From Here?" Online 5 (July 1981): 30-42. Design considerations for the future.

Faibisoff, Sylvia G. and Jitka Hurych. "Is There a Future for the End User in Online Bibliographic Searching?" Special Libraries 72 (October 1981): 347-55. The authors argue that many end users will want to search and librarians should educate them.

Haines, Judith S. "Experiences in Training End-User Searchers." Online 6 (November 1982): 14-23.

Janke, Richard V. "BRS/After Dark: The Birth of Online Self-Service." Online 7 (September 1983): 12-30. Winner of the 1983 Data Courier-Online Inc. Best Online Article award.

Janke, Richard V. "Online After Six: End User Searching Comes of Age." Online 8 (November 1984): 15-29. Follow-up on earlier article. Excellent bibliography.

WILLIAMS, MARTHA E. "Electronic Databases." Science 228 (26 April 1985): 445-56.

Although this article is aimed at a broad audience and assumes no prior knowledge of online searching, it is a valuable state-of-the-art summary for all. Williams is a pioneer and recognized leader in the field of online literature searching. In this article she defines databases in detail, differentiating between word-oriented, number-oriented, and picture-oriented. Word-oriented databases are further defined as bibliographic and full text. Specific examples are given throughout. Access to databases through online search service organizations is described with 1984 or 1985 data.

In addition to the descriptive information, Williams addresses several issues in online searching today. This is a good article to go to for definitions and short discussions of user-friendly front-end software, gateway systems, and artificial intelligence techniques in online searching. Other issues and trends discussed include: the conflict between low-priced public-sector databases and their commercial competitors, transborder data flow, copyright and downloading, optical disk technology for locally-held databases, and the changing role of publishers.

No other article to date tackles such an ambitious summary of past, present, and future issues in online searching. It also presents the viewpoints of intermediary searchers, end-user searchers, database publishers, and online service organizations.

Williams is professor of information science, University of Illinois, Champaign-Urbana.

Related reading

Bourne, Charles P. "On-Line Systems: History, Technology, and Economics." Journal of the American Society for Information Science 31 (May 1980): 156-60.

Hawkins, Donald T. "On-Line Information Retrieval Bibliography, 1964-1979." Marlton, NJ: Learned Information, Inc., 1980. Updated every year in the April issue of Online Review.

Shroder, Emelie J. "Online Reference Service: How to Begin--A Selected Bibliography." RQ 22 (Fall 1982): 70-75. Reprinted in James J. Maloney, ed., Online Searching Technique and Management. Chicago: American Library Association, 1983.

Tenopir, Carol. "Full-Text Databases." Annual Review of Information Science and Technology" 19 (1984): 215-46. Overview of full-text databases and research on their use.

Wanger, Judith and Ruth N. Landau. "Nonbibliographic On-Line Data Base Services." Journal of the American Society for Information Science 31 (May 1980): 171-80.

BATES, MARCIA J. "Information Search Tactics." Journal of the American Society for Information Science 30 (July 1979): 205-14.

Winner of the 1979 award for best paper published in the Journal of the American Society for Information Science, this is a scholarly treatment of search tactics for professional searchers. Twenty-nine specific "tactics", defined as strategies or moves "that will improve the effectiveness and efficiency of an online search", are drawn from the literature, the author's experience, and her observations of professional searchers.

Bates divides the 29 tactics into four broad categories: 1) monitoring tactics to keep the search efficient, 2) file structure tactics to make best use of the database and search system characteristics, 3) search formulation tactics to design and control the search process, and 4) term tactics to select and revise specific terms to be searched.

Specific tactics range from the mundane (for example, RESPELL to search under a different spelling or CORRECT to watch for and correct spelling and factual errors), to the complex (for example, SURVEY to review at each decision point the available options or STRETCH to use a source for a purpose other than that intended), to the humorous (for example, BIBBLE to look for a bibliography already prepared, "before launching oneself into the effort of preparing one.")

There is a tactic here for every situation and for every intermediary searcher. The article also is an attempt to begin to develop logical rules for the often intuitive process of search strategy and development. For those who may have trouble converting Bates' tactics to actual online situations, the more practical article by Hawkins listed below is recommended.

Bates was associate professor, University of Washington, School of Librarianship, Seattle, when the article was written and is now at the University of California at Los Angeles, Graduate School of Library and Information Science.

Related reading

Bates, Marcia J. "Search Techniques." Annual Review of Information Science and Technology 16 (1981): 139-69. A review of research on search strategy and techniques.

Fenichel, Carol Hansen. "The Process of Searching Online Bibliographic Databases: A Review of Research." Library Research 2 (Summer 1980): 107-27.

Hawkins, Donald T. and Robert Wagers. "Online Bibliographic Search Strategy Development." Online 6 (May 1982): 12-19.

Knapp, Sarah. "The Reference Interview in the Computer-Based Setting." RQ 17 (Summer 1978): 320-24.

LYNCH, MARY JO. Financing Online Search Services in Publicly
Supported Libraries: The Report of an ALA Survey. Chicago:
American Library Association, 1981. Summarized in: Lynch, Mary
Jo. "Libraries Embrace Online Search Fees." American Libraries
14 (March 1982): 174.

This often-cited research report on how public libraries
finance online search services provides valuable information for
decision making. The bulk of the report describes a survey sent
by ALA via the major online vendors to publicly supported
libraries. Results were tabulated and interpreted by the Library
Research Center at the Graduate School of Library and Information
Science, University of Illinois at Champaign-Urbana.

Libraries were asked to respond to a series of questions
regarding fees for online services. The results showed that most
libraries charge for online searching, but only on a cost-recovery
basis. A majority of respondents believed that users, searchers,
and administrators had positive feelings about the financing
method, whether or not fees were charged.

The ALA has strongly advocated free access to all services in
public libraries and an appendix in this report reproduces the
"ALA Position Statement on Free Access to Information." Despite
ALA's position, this research report shows that in reality most
libraries charge some kind of fee for online searching. It is an
issue that is likely to be debated for many more years to come.

The report includes an analysis of the literature on fees for
online services and an extensive bibliography.

Lynch is director, Office for Research, American Library
Association.

Related reading

Beeler, Richard J. and Antoinette L. Lueck. "Pricing of Online
Services for Nonprimary Clientele." The Journal of Academic
Librarianship 10 (May 1984): 69-72. Results of a survey of
differential charges by type of patron in academic libraries.

Boyce, Bert R. "A Cost Accounting Model for Online Computerized
Literature Searching." Journal of Library Administration 4
(Summer 1983): 43-49.

Buhman, Lesley. "Fee-For-Information: Legal, Social, and Economic
Implications." Journal of Library Administration 4 (Summer 1983):
1-10.

Drinan, Helen. "Financial Management of Online Services: A How to
Guide." Online 3 (October 1979): 14-21.

Linford, John. "To Charge or Not to Charge: A Rationale."
Library Journal 102 (October 1977): 2009-10.

WARRICK, THOMAS S. "Large Databases, Small Computers and Fast Modems...An Attorney Looks at the Legal Ramifications of Downloading." Online 8 (July 1984): 58-70.

Copyright of electronic databases has become an issue of concern with the widespread use of microcomputers for online searching. In addition to acting as a telecommunications device, microcomputers allow the searcher to capture search results on the computer's magnetic storage device (downloading).

Warrick presents the legal view of database downloading in light of the 1976 Copyright Law. No court has yet ruled on the database copyright issue, but some copyright principles clearly apply. Original works in a database are copyrightable. Bibliographic databases fall under the copyright provisions for collective works or compilations. Downloading of information in databases is clearly legal only when the provisions of fair use apply or if a not-for-profit library does it in a non-systematic way under the special copyright section for libraries.

Ultimately, there are "no hard and fast rules as to whether downloading is prohibited in all circumstances." Until the courts rule on the legality of downloading, lawyers such as Warrick can only use their best judgment to guess what an individual judge might rule. Regulating downloading by contract between the database producer and database user, by higher database fees, or by special legislation are given by Warrick as possible future solutions to the uncertainty.

Warrick is an attorney with the firm of Pierson Semmes Crolins and Finley, Washington, DC.

Related reading

Fenichel, Carol Hansen. "Using a Microcomputer to Communicate: Part 1: The Basics." Microcomputers for Information Management 2 (April 1985). What you need to get started using a microcomputer for online searching.

Jansen, Arnold A. "Problems and Challenges of Downloading for Database Producers." The Electronic Library 2 (January 1984): 41-51. The producer's viewpoint.

Miller, Jerome K. "Copyright Protection for Bibliographic, Numeric, Factual, and Textual Databases." Library Trends 32 (Fall 1983): 199-209.

Osborne, Larry N. "Downloading Overview." Journal of Library Administration (1985). Legal and ethical issues.

Tenopir, Carol. "Online Searching With A Microcomputer: Downloading Issues." Microcomputers for Information Management 2 (April 1985): 77-89. Summarizes surveys on downloading, contract and copyright issues, and future effects of downloading.

VIII

LIBRARY MANAGEMENT

The Landscape of Literature by PAUL METZ.
"Guide to Collection Evaluation Through Use and User Studies"
      by DOROTHY E. CHRISTIANSEN, C. ROGER DAVIS,
      and JUTTA REED-SCOTT.
"Collaborative Collection Development: Progress, Problems and
      Potential" by DAVID H. STAM,
"Library Patrons in an Age of Discontinuity" by C. LEE JONES.
"The Impact of Technology on Users of Academic Libraries"
      by C. LEE JONES.
"Interlibrary Loan Charges: The Arguments For and Against"
      by BASIL STUART-STUBBS and W. DENIS RICHARDSON.
"Periodical Prices: A History and Discussion" by ANN OKERSON.
The Economics of Research Libraries by MARTIN M. CUMMINGS.
Article on preservation from Humanities.
"Selection for Preservation: A Materialistic Approach"
      by ROSS ATKINSON.
"Cooperation in Preservation Microfilming." Three papers
      presented at an American Library Association program.
Report of the Committee on the Records of Government.
"Recon Trends" by JUTTA REED-SCOTT.

Related reading

"The Use and Misuse of Library User Studies" by HERBERT S. WHITE.
"It's So Easy to Use, Why Don't I Own it?" by HUGH ATKINSON.
Document Delivery in the United States
      by Information Systems Consultants Incorporated.
"Coordinating Collection Development: the RLG Conspectus"
      by NANCY E. GWINN and PAUL H. MOSHER.
"Library to Library" by ROD HENSHAW.
"Ownership Is Not Always Availability" by HERBERT S. WHITE.
"The Riddle of Journal Prices: What is Reported and What is
      Needed" from Scholarly Communication.
Economics of Academic Libraries
      by WILLIAM BAUMOL and MATITYAHU MARCUS.
"The Once and Future Preservation Crisis" by JAY WARD BROWN.
"Collection Development, Collection Management, and Preservation"
      by DAN C. HAZEN.
"Future of Microform in an Electronic Age"
      by CHARLES CHADWYCK-HEALEY.
"Toward Tomorrow: A Retrospective Conversion Project"
      by IRENE B. HOADLEY and LEILA PAYNE.

METZ, PAUL. <u>The Landscape of Literature</u>. Chicago: American
Library Association, 1983.

This provocative report of a study of library users calls
into question conventional collection development and organization
policies at academic libraries. Metz believes that libraries need
to examine closely their basic working assumptions. He argues
that policy is determined more often by narrow departmental
interests and unquestioned beliefs of librarians about who uses
what information and how, than by the actual needs and behaviors
of users. Because a library's particular structure strongly
influences the reading and research patterns of its users, Metz
believes that many libraries, by following inappropriate
collection policies, may not be adequately facilitating research
efforts.

On the basis of user and book circulation data collected over
a two-day period at a medium-sized academic library, Metz found
wide variation in research patterns among library users, depending
on their disciplinary affiliation and their level of subject
expertise.

The study Metz conducted found that:

1. Faculty and graduate students use the available
literature more intensively than other library users;
2. Scholars in the social sciences and to a lesser degree in
the humanities tend to rely more on books written outside their
own discipline than do scholars in the physical sciences;
3. Scientists make comparatively greater use of periodical
literature than do humanists and social scientists;
4. All researchers regardless of their discipline make
frequent use of outside literature; and
5. Most books are read principally by nonspecialists.

Since most research is interdisciplinary and most book users
are non-specialists, serious doubts are raised about the validity
of standard archival policy based on rigid compartmentalization of
disciplines and on the particular orientation and influence of
academic departments. Not only is the researcher ill-served by a
decentralized library system that scatters collections according
to discipline--typical of many university libraries--but he or she
is often additionally handicapped by the common library practice
of deferring collection development decisions to department
faculty who generally are ignorant of or indifferent to the needs
and desires of "nonspecialist" readers.

Metz makes a convincing case for libraries to follow a
centralized, interdisciplinary approach to document collection
relying less on faculty opinion and more on usage studies to
determine archival needs.

Metz is on the staff of the library at Virginia Polytechnic
Institute and State University.

CHRISTIANSEN, DOROTHY E., C. ROGER DAVIS and JUTTA REED-SCOTT. "Guide to Collection Evaluation Through Use and User Studies." Library Resources and Technical Services 27 (October/December 1983): 432-40.

"User studies" is the commonly used term for research on the ways people use libraries and perceive them. A number of types of user studies are listed in this guide; they include surveys of users' opinions, analysis of the circulation of books and book use inside the library, evaluation of the provision of materials (often called "document delivery"), assessments of the availability of books when they are needed, and studies of citations recorded by library users. The definitions, advantages, and disadvantages of each method are listed, and there are careful definitions of terms and methods. The article was compiled by a committee of the Resources and Technical Services Division of the American Library Association for those interested in evaluating library collections. The authors append a bibliography of examples of each type of study.

Christiansen is assistant director for reference services, University Libraries, SUNY at Albany; Davis is a bibliographer at Smith College Library; and Reed-Scott is collection development specialist at the Association of Research Libraries Office of Management Studies.

Related reading

White, Herbert S. "The Use and Misuse of Library User Studies." Library Journal 110 (December 1985): 70-71. White, who is dean of the library school at Indiana University, warns against being misled by the generally positive nature of opinion surveys, and cautions that users have been conditioned to accept minimal levels of service: "Fundamentally, this means that users ask for the library service they get and get the library service for which they ask." He points out that assessing users' real wants requires removing the constraints of budgets, time, and delivery mechanisms and allowing them to think freely about their ideals for information services. Advances in library services are unlikely to be achieved until users raise their sights and librarians respond to these greater challenges.

Atkinson, Hugh C. "It's so Easy to Use, Why Don't I Own It?" Library Journal 109 (1984): 1102-03.

Information Systems Consultants Inc. Document Delivery in the United States (October 1983; ERIC document ED244 626). Provides information on the Achilles heel of interlibrary loan: materials located and requested electronically frequently cannot be rapidly transported.

STAM, DAVID H. "Collaborative Collection Development: Progress, Problems and Potential." IFLA Journal 12 (1986): 9-19.

Founded in 1974, the Research Libraries Group has as part of its agenda the development of collaborative programs to address library needs. Its work in collection development draws together the 24 RLG members, the North American Collection Inventory Project sponsored by the Association of Research Libraries and the work of the Canadian Association of Research Libraries. Former chair of the RLG Collection Management and Development Committee, Stam describes the Conspectus developed by RLG to aid coordination of collecting activity. As an assessment tool, the Conspectus includes both collection strengths and current collecting commitments. The goal is to build upon strengths, identify weaknesses, and assign primary collecting responsibilities or commitments to maintain current strength in particular areas.

Stam outlines some of the difficulties participants have encountered in attempting to develop a unified approach to national collection development: the subjectivity of most assessments and attempts at objective assessments; organizational problems including interdisciplinary fields, format collections, language codes, and logistics; political considerations; and the wider implications for related operations such as document delivery, preservation, bibliographic control and communication. On the positive side, the conspectus provides a tool to increase interdependence and bring librarians together to consider national needs plus the ability to relate collection strengths to shared cataloging, retrospective conversion and preservation needs. It serves now as a basis for national planning in these areas, while also serving important local institutional needs.

Stam, former director of research libraries of the New York Public Library, is now director of the University of Syracuse Library.

Related reading

Gwinn, Nancy E. and Paul H. Mosher. "Coordinating Collection Development: The RLG Conspectus." College & Research Libraries News 44 (March 1983): 128-40.

JONES C. LEE. "Library Patrons in an Age of Discontinuity: Artifacts of Technology." Journal of Academic Librarianship 10 (1984): 151-54.

JONES C. LEE. "The Impact of Technology on Users of Academic Libraries." IFLA Journal 10 (1984): 49-56.

At a time when libraries are adopting technology at an increasing rate, librarians and researchers are trying to discover how users adapt to computerized services and how they will want to employ them. While a fully integrated library automated system is increasingly feasible, most libraries are automating their processes one by one. Searches of computerized bibliographic databases are offered by library reference departments, but only a small, although growing, proportion of users takes advantage of this service. Online catalogs that supplement and in time will replace card catalogs will affect a much larger percentage of users, and libraries are rapidly adopting them.

The online catalog is probably the most powerful force today because it has the potential for linking a variety of databases within the home institution and ultimately many far beyond the home institution. The Council on Library Resources (CLR) in 1980 funded a study of online catalogs to determine, in part, their impact on users. Findings reveal that users are enthusiastic and that the online catalog has changed both their behavior and their expectations of the library. However, there are no standards as yet for these systems, and users may find it frustrating to attempt to use different systems in different libraries. CLR is making efforts to increase librarians' and systems managers' awareness of this issue. Over time, users' habits in the use of microcomputers and telecommunications equipment will not only be affected by library technical developments but will influence them as well.

Jones is a consultant to the Council on Library Resources.

STUART-STUBBS, BASIL and W. DENIS RICHARDSON. "Interlibrary Loan
Charges: The Arguments For and Against." Interlending and
Document Supply 12 (January 1984): 3-10.

Interlibrary loan was established during the early twentieth
century and firmly based in the principle of reciprocity between
institutions. However, during the past two decades imbalances in
borrowing and lending transactions have raised questions about the
costs to the large libraries that have supplied many of the loans.
Investigations by the Association of Research Libraries during the
1970s resulted in a series of studies evaluating the costs of
interlibrary loans and possible mechanisms for reimbursing the
large net lending institutions. Many large libraries now levy
fees for loans, and these are often passed on to the individual
requesting the loan. A recent study by the ARL ("Interlibrary
Loan Survey," in Association of Research Libraries, Office of
Management Studies, Systems and Procedures Exchange Center,
Interlibrary Loan in ARL Libraries, SPEC Kit 92; Washington: ARL,
March 1983) established that an increasing number of libraries
charged fees for loan services. The Stuart-Stubbs and Richardson
statement of the pros and cons of fees states the usual arguments,
and may be enlightening to those who are interested in following
current opinion on this topic. The journal itself, Interlending
and Document Supply, is a British organ that summarizes
international trends in interlibrary loans. Its numerous articles
can help to put the complicated and constantly changing status of
interlibrary loan services into perspective.

Related reading

Henshaw, Rod. "Library to Library." Wilson Library Bulletin 59
(February 1985): 403, 431. For library users, interlibrary loan
often seems a complex process that involves long waiting and not
infrequent disappointments. While librarians often see it that
way as well, they are aware as few users are that online
bibliographic databases, the growth of bibliographic utilities,
and the emergence of commercial document vendors continue to
change the way the lending system works. Henshaw, who writes a
regular column for the Wilson Bulletin, refers to a few of these
changes in discussing the elements of interlibrary loan, beginning
with generally accepted practices and concluding with a discussion
of local state and regional resource-sharing programs and special
agreements. Noting that many of these effectively deny access by
charging high loan fees, he makes a plea for coordination and
planning at the national level to encourage better use of the
nation's library resources.

White, Herbert S. "Ownership Is Not Always Availability." In Sul
H. Lee, Access to Scholarly Information: Issues and Strategies.
Ann Arbor: Pierian Press, 1985: 1-11.

OKERSON, ANN. "Periodical Prices: A History and Discussion."
Advances In Serial Management 1 (1986):101-34.

Ann Okerson looks at the reasons for, and the libraries'
response to, the rapid increase in serial prices over the last 15
years. Major indexes show that, overall, journal prices have
increased by over five times between 1970 and 1985--far outpacing
price increases in the rest of the economy.

The author finds little, if any, correlation between journal
prices and inflation. The high and rapidly rising periodical
prices are attributable to increased costs of journal production,
greater length of the average journal, a declining number of
subscriptions, which lead publishers to raise prices in order to
recover lost revenue, and finally, to pricing practices, such as
dual-pricing, that discriminate against libraries.

Libraries are beginning to respond to hikes in journal costs
in a variety of ways, such as undertaking user studies of in-house
subscriptions, cancelling or limiting seldom used periodicals,
using InterLibrary Loan and online services rather than relying
exclusively on in-house collections, and speaking out against
unfair pricing practices by publishers and subscription agents.

Libraries have been particularly outspoken about dual
pricing. While most libraries accept publishers' arguments that
a library should be charged more than an individual for a
subscription since it serves a greater number of readers, they
object to the vast discrepancy in individual and library rates,
for which they find no reasonable justification. Okerson cites a
library survey of medical journals which found an average price
differential of 102.4 percent between individual and library
subscription prices.

Libraries are most upset over geographically-based price
differentiation, the long-standing European practice of charging
significantly higher prices to American and Canadian clients than
to domestic buyers.

Okerson believes that through use of price indexes, automated
accounting systems, stricter selection of subscriptions, and
greater communication with publishers, libraries will be better
able to control their serial budgets without seriously
compromising archival needs. She cites several areas for further
research: how to control nonperiodical serial budgets; how to
adapt existing price indexes to local situations; how to use
automated accounting systems in predicting serials; and how to
correlate journal inflation figures and the Consumer Price Index.

Okerson is head of the Library Serials Division of Simon
Fraser University in British Columbia.

Related reading

"The Riddle of Journal Prices: What is Reported and What is
Needed." Scholarly Communication no. 2 (Fall 1985): 11.

CUMMINGS, MARTIN M. The Economics of Research Libraries.
Washington, D.C.: Council on Library Resources, 1986.

In 1982, the Council on Library Resources began a two-year
study of the economics of research libraries, headed by Dr. Martin
M. Cummings. Drawing on the expertise of a group of librarians,
university administrators, consultants, library school faculty,
and others, CLR held three seminars on the subject, commissioned
several studies, and held a series of mini-seminars at seven
universities. From these experiences and a comprehensive review
of the literature of library economics, Cummings produced this
report. While it builds on the standard work on the topic by
Baumol and Marcus, it is a fundamentally different kind of work,
just as the library situation differs greatly today. In fact,
this work provides a view of the constraints and opportunities
oddly juxtaposed in available new technologies and static or
declining budgets; it is a description of libraries in transition
to a future that as yet is not clear to the principal actors.

Cummings documents carefully the great lacunae in available
data sources and calls for better management information systems,
more cost and performance studies, and improved communication
between librarians and institutional officers, but he recognizes
that these are not the only needs. He is aware that much of the
future depends on executive vision and institutional climate, upon
leadership and expertise. The book provides details about library
finance and trends in it that are not generally understood outside
the profession, and understood but dimly within it. It is helpful
to those wishing to understand why libraries stand at a
technological and financial crossroads.

Cummings, a library consultant, was formerly the director of
the National Library of Medicine.

Related reading

Baumol, William, and Matityahu Marcus. Economics of Academic
Libraries. Washington, D.C.: American Council on Education, 1973.

"Preservation." Humanities 6 (August 1985): 26-36.

The enormous tasks that face those engaged in library preservation programs are not yet well understood. A new Office of Preservation was created at the National Endowment for the Humanities in 1985 to encourage work in this area and enhance awareness of the difficulties involved, and this section of its magazine is devoted to describing the magnitude of preservation needs and discussing existing programs. The first director of the NEH Office, Harold Cannon, provides a general introduction, underscoring the need for careful selection of items to be preserved. Two projects, the National Newspaper Project, and the American Philological Associations's review of classical works, are highlighted. (The full report of the Philological Society project is annotated in section IX). Margaret Child, Smithsonian Institution Libraries, discusses new techniques such as preservation microfilming, optical digital disks, and paper deacidification. Mass storage, she emphasizes, will continue to be primarily on microform, but users will not experience the difficulties that microform use caused in the past because automated retrieval will ease the problem of providing access. Additional articles describe the Research Libraries Group Cooperative Preservation Microfilming Project and the Wisconsin Conservation Service Center's training programs that prepare nonprofessionals to handle simple preservation techniques.

While the subject of preservation has not been of great interest to scholars in the past, this series makes the case that the world of scholarship needs to become closely involved with efforts to save our heritage. Those who are beginning their efforts to understand the problems and needs in their own fields may find it provides a useful starting point.

Related reading

Brown, Jay Ward. "The Once and Future Preservation Crisis." Wilson Library Bulletin 59 (May 1985): 591-96. Brown provides an introductory look at the preservation problem, reviewing the causes, the statistics of book deterioration, and the obstacles that confront librarians. Paper manufacturers have been reluctant to convert to alkaline processes and publishers frequently do not find it advantageous to purchase acid-free paper; in the absence of public concern, librarians are trying to foster official interest by instituting standards for book paper. They also are trying to combat the problem by using deacidification processes, microfilming brittle books, and converting information to electronic form. The difficulty with these methods is that they are costly and many library budgets cannot include such expenses. Public interest in and involvement with the preservation crisis might help to change some of these conditions. But as Brown makes clear, the solutions are not yet at hand.

ATKINSON, ROSS. "Selection for Preservation: A Materialistic
Approach." Library Resources and Technical Services 30 (October-
December 1986): 341-53.

Ross Atkinson sees preservation policy as inextricably linked
with that of collection development and believes it should be
formulated according to similar criteria. Two fundamental
decisions must be made: what should be preserved and what mode of
preservation should be used.

Atkinson builds his preservation methodology on the basis of
a three-tiered classification of materials.

Class 1 consists of materials of high economic value, such as
rare books and manuscripts, and comprehensive collections.
Atkinson recommends that all Class 1 documents receive first
priority in preservation selection, with restoration as the
preferred preservation method. As the criteria for selection of
Class 1 documents are primarily economic, Atkinson recommends that
preservation decisions be made at the local institutional level.

Class 2 includes all materials in high demand and expected to
remain in high demand. Here, Atkinson considers reprinting and
photocopying the most appropriate preservation options and the
local library the appropriate arbiter in preservation decisions.

Class 3 encompasses all other materials. Having no
overriding "legitimizing" characteristic--that is, high economic
value or high user demand, Class 3 documents pose a difficult
preservation dilemma for librarians. Atkinson sees a cooperative,
nationally coordinated program as the only viable way to handle
Class 3 materials. Such a program, Atkinson argues, must meet the
following requirements: (a) it must provide future scholars a
representative collection of documents; (b) it must be
economically practicable; (c) it must be politically acceptable;
(d) it must be designed to allow for indefinite expansion; and (e)
it must be put into effect very soon.

Atkinson proposes that libraries collectively determine the
strongest collection in each subject area and designate it as the
"collection of record." Collections would be preserved on
microfilm by the holding institution, and linked together by a
shared bibliographic database to form a balanced and integrated
"community of documentation." He believes such a program could be
easily implemented and that it would place no undue financial
strain on any institution.

Atkinson is assistant university librarian for collection
development at the University of Iowa.

Related reading

Hazen, Dan C. "Collection Development, Collection Management, and
Preservation." Library Resources and Technical Services 26
(January-March 1982): 6-10.

"Cooperation in Preservation Microfilming." Three papers presented at the Resources and Technical Services Division, ALA, Preservation Microfilming Committee Program, June 25, 1984. Library Resources and Technical Services 29 (January-March 1985): 80-101.

According to Nancy Gwinn's paper, "The Rise and Fall of Cooperative Projects," preservation microfilming began as early as 1938. Except for brief declines in the 1950s and early 1970s, microfilming has continued since that time to ensure that important research materials can be retained. Most preservation projects of the 1980s deal with carefully defined classes of material, are carefully coordinated, and have attracted foundation support. Major actors in these efforts are the National Endowment for the Humanities, the Research Libraries Group, and several professional associations.

William J. Welsh, in "The Library of Congress: A More-Than-Equal Partner," describes the role of LC in preservation, stressing efforts to provide bibliographic control, microfilm items in the LC collections, develop and share technical tools and methods, and research new solutions to preservation problems.

Margaret S. Child writes in "The Future of Cooperative Preservation Microfilming" that "microfilm is currently the best option we have" for preserving library materials, and stresses that it is important not to delay filming even though some feel that technological breakthroughs are imminent. While much is being done by individual institutions, national coordination is essential. Elements of a national program such as standards for filming, and bibliographical control are in place or evolving, but attention to such needs as regional centers, training, public education, and an information exchange has become essential. The Council on Library Resources, long interested in preservation, has led an effort to develop a national strategy for coordinating efforts to preserve brittle books.

Related reading

Chadwyck-Healey, Charles. "The Future of Microform in an Electronic Age." Wilson Library Bulletin 58 (December 1983): 270-73. A microform publisher himself, Chadwyck-Healey is well qualified to evaluate the advantages and limitations of microforms and their utility for an automated age. While his conclusion in favor of microforms for most current applications can be anticipated, he also takes a careful look at the alternatives and discusses the choices made by publishers in terms of the economics of reproducing specialized research materials. He observes that applications in videodisk publishing are likely to be in areas not covered through microform publication, and recommends that librarians take a cautious approach to the new technologies.

Committee on the Records of Government. <u>Report</u>. Washington, D.C., March 1985. Distributed by the Council on Library Resources.

Sponsored by the Council on Library Resources, the American Council of Learned Societies, and the Social Science Research Council, the Committee conducted an eighteen-month investigation of the issues facing public archives. Its mission was to identify and propose methods that governments at all levels can use to eliminate unneeded records while ensuring preservation of the small proportion that deserve to be kept. While existing paper records consume extensive space, word processing technology makes it easy to erase text and rapid changes in technology mean that electronic records may no longer be readable within short periods of time. Among the topics considered were methods of organizing, storing, and preserving government records; the unique challenges posed by computer-generated records; employment of new technologies in records management; and public expectations for access to the contents of archival institutions. The report summarizes the Committee's work, conclusions, and recommendations, concluding with a proposed text for a presidential executive order to systematize record keeping activities throughout the federal government. Appendices include an overview of government records programs, a discussion of conservation problems, and a National Archives report on technology assessment. Additional information on government regulations and legislation and on regulations, principles, and guidelines for record agencies follows the text.

REED-SCOTT, JUTTA. "Recon Trends." <u>American Libraries</u> 16 (November 1985): 694-700.

Retrospective conversion is the process of putting catalog records for parts or all of the library's collection into an online database. This makes it possible, in theory, to dispense with the card catalog entirely. Many libraries have undertaken RECON projects since the mid- to late 1970s. Reed-Scott, who conducted the Association of Research Libraries Retrospective Conversion Planning Study, provides a review of the trend to RECON. She describes the process, the products, and available options for conducting RECON projects. She also outlines the initiatives that have helped shape the current coordinated strategy and program by the ARL to convert all bibliographic records for monographs not yet in machine-readable format. Predicting that RECON will grow rapidly during the next five to seven years, due to the pressures to automate and the fact that small libraries will undertake conversion efforts, Reed-Scott documents her assertions with a list of available resources and grant funding provided for projects. By the mid-1990s, according to her timetable, "all but a few of the largest research libraries will have completed the conversion for their collections...The agenda for the future will be to build links among libraries and to expand cooperative programs."

Reed-Scott is collection development specialist in the Association of Research Libraries Office of Management.

Related reading

Hoadley, Irene B. and Leila Payne. "Toward Tomorrow: A Retrospective Conversion Project." <u>Journal of Academic Librarianship</u> 9 (July 1983): 138-41.

IX

RESEARCH AND SCHOLARSHIP

"The Life of Learning" by MAYNARD MACK.
"The ACLS Survey of Scholars: Views on Publications, Computers,
    Libraries" by HERBERT C. MORTON and ANNE JAMIESON PRICE.
"Progress in Documentation: Invisible Colleges and Information
    Transfer, a Review and Commentary with Particular Reference
    to the Social Sciences" by BLAISE CRONIN.
A Difficult Balance: Editorial Peer Review in Medicine
    by STEPHEN LOCK.
"Journal Peer Review: The Need for a Research Agenda"
    by JOHN BAILAR and KAY PATTERSON
"On Academic Authorship" by DONALD KENNEDY.
"Involving Scholars in Preservation Decisions: The Case of the
    Classicists" by ROGER S. BAGNALL and CAROLYN L. HARRIS
"Data Banks for the Humanities: Learning from Thesaurus Linguae
    Graecae" by THEODORE BRUNNER.
"A Reconsideration of Manuscript Editing" by ELEANOR HARMAN.

Related reading

The Humanities in American Life: Report of the Commission on the
    Humanities.
Invisible Colleges: Diffusion of Knowledge in Scientific
    Communities by D. CRANE.
"Scientific Communication: Five Themes from Sociology"
    by H. MENZEL.
Science Since Babylon by D. J. DeSOLLA PRICE.
"Collaboration in an Invisible College"
    by D. J. DeSOLLA PRICE and B. DE. BEAVER.
"Peer Review and Public Policy"
    from Science, Technology and Human Values.
"Patterns of Evaluation in Science: Institutionalization,
    Structure and Functions of the Referee System"
    by H. ZUCKERMAN and ROBERT K. MERTON.
"On Being an Uncompromising Editor" by J. G. BELL.
Editors on Editing: An Inside View of What Editors Really Do
    by GERALD GROSS.
"Looking at the Last dollar" by IAN MONTAGNES.
"Training Professional Editors for Scientific Journals"
    by F. PETER WOODFORD.

MACK, MAYNARD. "The Life of Learning," <u>ACLS Newsletter</u>, 34
(Winter-Spring 1983): 2-15.

The Charles Homer Haskins Lectures were established by the
American Council of Learned Societies in 1983 to give leading
scholars an opportunity to offer their reflections on the "life of
learning." The inaugural lecture, by Maynard Mack, is notable not
only for its ideas and convictions, but equally for the felicity
with which the thoughts are expressed--scholarly communication at
its best.

Mack singles out three topics for comment--prospects for the
humanities, what ever happened to teaching, and "the academy:
verdict not in." It is in the second part that he addresses
directly two aspects of scholarly communication, overemphasis on
"published scholarship" and the failure to communicate with the
community outside the campus.

"To study, to keep learning, to read widely and
reflectively: these pursuits are essential to our profession, it
goes without saying. I believe, too, that it is crucial to one's
intellectual vitality to try to write (when one has something to
write worth writing)....But the qualifying clause is essential:
one is to write when one has something to write worth writing."

The present system, he believes, penalizes those--"often our
very best"--who are "unwilling to measure out their minds in
three-year book-length sections," and encourages seasoned scholars
to blow up into mediocre treatises what would have been acceptable
essays.

Too few scholars, in Mack's view, are willing to share their
learning with a wider public, "an activity that would peculiarly
become us as 'humanists,'" for fear of being called popularizers.
He calls on scholars to find ways to communicate with a far larger
public than they do now.

If he were a graduate dean, Mack adds, he would insist that
students not only turn out an acceptable dissertation but also a
publishable essay that would reach a larger audience. "It takes
much harder work to write for the public than to write for one's
colleagues. And it has a cleansing effect on one's vocabulary."

Mack is Sterling Professor of English, Emeritus, Yale
University.

Related reading

<u>The Humanities in American Life: Report of the Commission on the
Humanities</u>. Berkeley and Los Angeles: University of California
Press, 1980.

MORTON, HERBERT C. and ANNE JAMIESON PRICE. "The ACLS Survey of Scholars: Views on publications, computers, libraries." Scholarly Communication no. 5 (Summer 1986): 1-16.

What do scholars in the humanities and social sciences read and write? How do they use computers? What are their views on a wide variety of issues from peer review to the quality of library collections and services? In late 1985 the Office of Scholarly Communication of the American Council of Learned Societies surveyed more than 5,000 members of ACLS societies to get some answers to questions such as these. About 71 percent of those in the sample responded to the questionnaires, which suggests that scholars are willing to take the time to respond to inquiries about their needs and concerns (the questionnaires took 30 to 40 minutes to complete) and that the issues encompassed by the phrase "scholarly communication" are of importance to them.

Among the major findings:

Computer use has risen rapidly. The number of respondents who either owned a personal computer or had one for their exclusive use rose from 2 percent in 1980 to 45 percent in 1985.

More than 20 percent of all respondents consider informal publication, prepublication distribution of articles by their colleagues, to be at least as important to them as articles read in journals.

Three out of four respondents think the peer review system for journals in their field is biased; nearly half say reform is needed.

More than half of the respondents consider the interlibrary loan to be of great or moderate importance.

An overwhelming percentage of respondents think that the long-run effect of computers on research in their discipline will be positive.

The survey results also indicated that nearly one respondent in six is a scholar working outside the campus--in government, business, private research institutions, and secondary school teaching, or is self-employed. These scholars remain active, participate in scholarly associations, and contribute to the scholarly literature, though on the average they write fewer publications than their academic colleagues.

Morton is director and Price is staff associate of the Office of Scholarly Communication and Technology.

CRONIN, BLAISE. "Progress in Documentation: Invisible Colleges and Information Transfer, a Review and Commentary with Particular Reference to the Social Sciences." Journal of Documentation 38 (September 1982): 212-36.

The "invisible college," an ingroup of researchers who routinely communicate informally, has been a target of study since the term was first introduced in 1961 by Derek J. De Solla Price. Cronin summarizes these studies noting that an invisible college is not always present, but is "an optional feature of a developing research field or an ancillary communication conduit in a mature discipline."

Informal communication is termed "the lifeblood of scientific progress for both the physical and social sciences". The invisible college exists because it serves the needs of the academic community--often providing research ideas, facilitating formulation of research problems, and encouraging the rapid communication of innovative ideas. Whether it will be transformed with the advent of electronic networks remains to be seen. Cronin discusses the advantages and disadvantages of the invisible college and says that, in spite of its shortcomings, it "is likely to remain a pivotal feature of the scientific communication system for the foreseeable future." He recommends ways to take advantage of its benefits and suggests several avenues for further research.

This article is based on a report commissioned by the British Library Research and Development Department.

Cronin is a member of the Aslib Research and Consultancy Division.

Related reading

Crane, Diana. Invisible Colleges: Diffusion of Knowledge in Scientific Communities. Chicago: University of Chicago Press, 1972.

Menzel, H. "Scientific Communication: Five Themes from Sociology." (1966) Reprinted in B. C. Griffith, ed., Key Papers in Information Science. Washington: American Society for Information Science, 1980: 58-63.

Price, D. J. De Solla. Science Since Babylon. New Haven: Yale University Press, 1961.

Price, D. J. De Solla and B. De. Beaver "Collaboration in an Invisible College." American Psychologist 21 (1966): 1011-17.

LOCK, STEPHEN. A Difficult Balance: Editorial Peer Review in Medicine. Philadelphia: ISI Press, 1986.

This is the most comprehensive and useful assessment yet made of editorial peer review in journals. It was originally published in London as the 1985 Rock Carling Fellowship monograph and then made available in the United States by the Institute for Scientific Information. Lock reviews the extensive but rather inchoate literature in the field (281 references), reports his own study of peer review at the British Medical Journal, where he is editor, and assesses the need for further knowledge and investigation. Overall, he concludes that peer review is a useful and indispensable institution, but needs to be improved.

Lock divides criticism of peer review into two groups: process and outcome. The process, for example, has been called too costly by some editors. It has also been called biased. Among the studies pointing to this conclusion, Lock reviews a 1982 study reporting how a dozen published articles in psychology, chosen at random, were resubmitted to the same journals with cosmetic changes to disguise their identity. Eight of the 12 were rejected the second time around. Criticisms of this study and rejoinders have generated a substantial literature.

Outcome failures include the inability of referees to spot articles that were previously published, statistical errors in published work, plagiarism, and fraud.

Lock's own empirical study covers every article submitted to the British Medical Journal from January 1 to August 15, 1979. He reviews the recommendations of referees, decisions by the editor, the proportion of studies that were revised in the light of the decisions by referees, the fate of the articles rejected (published elsewhere as submitted, published elsewhere after substantial revision, remaining unpublished).

While Lock concludes that journal peer review does lead to better decisions on what to publish and improvements in what is published, he thinks a number of improvements can be made. He considers the prime responsibility to be the editor's since the editor must establish standards for selecting referees, provide guidelines for assessments to the referees and monitor the process. He reminds us, too, that some defects are inherent. The system must be judged by reasonable standards if the suggestions for "betterment" are to be realistic and effective.

Related reading

"Peer Review and Public Policy," a special issue of Science, Technology and Human Values 10 (Summer 1985). A broad examination of the subject covering not only journal articles but also the evaluation of research proposals submitted for government funding and the evaluation and interpretation of research findings for policymaking.

BAILAR, JOHN and KAY PATTERSON. "Journal Peer Review: The Need for a Research Agenda." New England Journal of Medicine 312 (March 7, 1985): 654-57.

Despite the central role of peer review in scholarly communication, little is known about its effectiveness. The authors review the literature on the subject in the sciences and conclude that "little sound scientific work has been published on journal peer review, and serious gaps may not be filled soon or in a technically acceptable fashion unless special efforts are made." They found that none of the studies conducted over the past ten years were based on a random sample of journals, and only a dozen were designed to test a specific hypothesis or examine a specific issue, or were based on a clearly designed sample. In addition to the methodological weaknesses, the authors point out that most studies emphasize the process rather than the outcomes.

Current attitudes toward peer review are reflected in the following statements: (1) the system screens out worthy from unworthy submissions; (2) peer review's principal function is to determine where an article gets published, since a determined author can almost always get the work published; (3) peer review leads to improvements in the quality of manuscripts; and (4) the results of peer review are essentially unpredictable.

Our inability to determine on the basis of available evidence which of these, or combination of them, best describes the current scene points to the need for further research. Bailar and Patterson call for "a thorough analysis of journal peer-review policy and of relevant research needs" to be conducted over the next decade or two under the auspices of some group or agent, with the cooperation of editors, authors and referees--and the assistance of professional societies. Some of the topics worth investigating are: (1) the costs of peer review, (2) the efficacy of "blind reviewing," (3) the efficacy of different types of instructions to referees, and (4) tracking manuscripts from inception to final disposition. (Many of these topics are covered in the context of the experience of a single journal in Stephen Lock's study, described in this bibliography).

Bailar and Patterson conclude that despite the shortcomings they identify, they retain a high regard for the system and know of no feasible alternative.

Related reading

Zuckerman, H. and Robert K. Merton. "Patterns of Evaluation in Science: Institutionalization, Structure and Functions of the Referee System." Minerva 9 (1971): 66-100.

KENNEDY, DONALD. "On Academic Authorship". Letter to members of
the Academic Council, Stanford University, September 18, 1985.
(Also available as Reprint 4, Office of Scholarly Commmunication).

The President of Stanford University, Donald Kennedy,
addresses the increasingly complex problem of assessing and
assigning credit and responsibility for academic works. Kennedy
notes the rising incidence of academic fraud and unethical
behavior in regard to authorship, and attributes it largely to
three factors: the growing complexity of research projects, often
involving large numbers of independent researchers; increasing
departmental pressure on faculty to publish frequently; and to the
significant reduction in scholars' research and writing time as a
result of increased administrative tasks.

Kennedy believes that new, general standards for intellectual
ownership need to be established. He concedes that such standards
would be difficult to determine as disputes over proper credit and
citation more often hinge on differences of personal values and
etiquette than on questions of legality and constitutionality, but
feels they could nevertheless serve as guiding norms for scholarly
research and publication.

Academic departments must inform their members and students
of existing authorship rules so as to minimize opportunities for
misunderstanding or misconduct. Kennedy cites the common case of
the collaborating student who expects official acknowledgement of
his contribution to published research findings only to discover
later that his supervising faculty does not. Such confusion over
authorship often leads to student complaints.

Kennedy also recognizes, however, that many student
grievances stem from misunderstandings not only by students, but
also by faculty members, who often misjudge the true purpose and
proper function of student research assistants. Kennedy points
out the important role that students can play in the advancement
of scholarly research, and calls on the faculty to view and use
students not only as assistants, but as colleagues to whom proper
credit is due.

Because authorship of collaborative work is so difficult to
determine, Kennedy suggests that authorship be granted to any
collaborator who can effectively defend the project with which he
is involved at a professional meeting, and that collaborating
authors share full and equal credit and responsibility unless
indicated otherwise.

In his closing remarks, Kennedy questions the emphasis on
requiring faculty to publish frequently, which he maintains has
both encouraged academic misconduct as well as led to a
"pathological growth" of publications, often of doubtful quality.
By placing less importance on publication as a criterion for
professional advancement and by revising current criteria for
academic authorship, Kennedy believes that the academic community
will be better able to maintain its traditionally high standards
of intellectual and moral excellence.

BAGNALL, ROGER S. and CAROLYN L. HARRIS. "Involving Scholars in Preservation Decisions: The Case of the Classicists." Journal of Academic Librarianship 13 (July 1987).

This account of an innovative and highly successful project describes what is probably the first major effort by a scholarly discipline to take a direct hand in preserving its own literature. Traditionally, librarians have taken the lead in dramatizing the preservation issue, in preserving deteriorating items in their own collections, and in developing strategies for coordinated nationwide preservation programs--drawing in scholars as it seemed appropriate to do so. By and large, scholars have been on the sidelines, and questions about how scholars can contribute and how much they should be involved remain unanswered.

In 1984 the American Philological Association received grants to preserve on microfiche the contents of the most important materials in classical studies published between 1850 and 1914 and to provide access to them. This was the period in which publishers began to use cheap, highly acidic paper, which is already crumbling or deteriorating rapidly.

The APA set up an editorial board of seven specialists in different aspects of classical studies to assist in selecting what to preserve. The choices were made title-by-title--in contrast to the more typical practice of preserving entire collections or portions of collections because title-by-title decisions can be prohibitively time-consuming and costly.

The authors describe how the selection process worked, how it might be improved, and the lessons they want to pass on to other scholars and librarians engaged in preservation projects. They found that scholars do not agree among themselves on the question whether everything should be preserved. Scholars also are very reluctant to see disbinding and discarding of books for microfilming even if the copies are crumbling.

The project succeeded in preserving on microfilm 25-30 percent of the 20,000 volumes of classics material (excluding dissertations) published during this period--thus capturing the most important of the vulnerable literature. Much of it will be available inexpensively on microfiche for purchase by both libraries and scholars. Revenue from sales will be used to help continue the preservation work.

The authors believe that their experience indicates that in some areas title-by-title selection by scholars is not unmanageable, even though they encountered many problems both in producing the microfiche and in using scholars' time efficiently. They also believe that the need for preservation microfilming should be explained to scholars in order to gain their support.

Bagnall is chairman of the Department of Classics at Columbia University and Harris is head of the Preservation Division, Columbia University Library.

BRUNNER, THEODORE. "Data Banks for the Humanities: Learning from Thesaurus Linguae Graecae." Scholarly Communication no. 7 (Winter 1987): 1, 6-9.

The founder of the Thesaurus Linguae Graecae data bank (TLG)--the world's most comprehensive electronic data bank of classical Greek literature--discusses its creation and offers advice to other data bank designers and administrators in the humanities.

Requiring 12 years and $6 million to create, the TLG contains two-thirds of all known existing Greek texts dating from Homer (about 750 B.C.) to 600 A.D., over 60 million words of text. Completing the project required vast intellectual and scholarly resources as well as the guidance and support of the entire discipline. TLG turned to private donors, foundations and federal agencies for financial assistance. Brunner stresses the importance of outside financial support in creating and maintaining any large data bank and exhorts data bank planners to give high priority to fundraising and public relations activities.

Brunner urges planners to be flexible and experimental when designing and creating data banks. With today's rapidly changing computer technology, Brunner believes data bank projects must be easily modifiable if they are to remain viable in the long run, and he points out a number of the technological and operational changes that the TLG has been required to undergo since its inception in 1972. Brunner also encourages planners to consider a variety of data entry methods before making a final choice. For example, he found optical scanning unsatisfactory for his purposes and in-house data entry less accurate and more expensive than data entry by commercial contractors in the Far East.

Brunner also addresses legal and economic issues such as copyright law, long-term financing, and product pricing and availability. He stresses the need for expert legal counsel in dealing with copyright issues but questions the supposed economic threat data banks pose to publishers. To the contrary, publishers' sales of classical Greek literature have increased since the creation of TLG. A far more real threat, Brunner argues, is the financial failure of data banks themselves. In contrast to a printed book, a data bank has ongoing operational costs that must be recovered either through user fees or external financing, which is difficult to obtain.

No ready answers are offered to such questions as how to safeguard data from misuse or illicit appropriation. Instead Brunner recommends these issues be settled through negotiation among all data bank participants and interest groups.

While acknowledging the range of problems that have yet to be solved, Brunner is encouraged by the steady increase in the number of classical scholars now making use of the Thesaurus Linguae Graecae. He believes that the TLG has led to increased and higher quality classical research and predicts that the TLG will lead to the creation of other data banks in the humanities.

HARMAN, ELEANOR. "A Reconsideration of Manuscript Editing."
Scholarly Publishing 7 (January 1976): 146-56.

Editing has become increasingly professional, and the need
for it is generally recognized.

The author considers compromise the essential element of
editing in order to maintain a balance among standards of the
publisher, the needs of the discipline, and the desires of the
writer. Editors are offered several reminders: beware indulging
personal linguistic or stylistic whims; remember that
perfectionism can be costly to the publisher; beware of extensive
rewriting, which can perpetuate a kind of fraud, making the writer
look better than he or she actually is.

Adapted from a paper presented at the 1975 annual meeting of
the Council of Biology Editors, Inc.

Eleanor Harman, formerly associate director of the University
of Toronto Press was the first editor of Scholarly Publishing.

Related reading

Bell, J. G. "On Being an Uncompromising Editor." Scholarly
Publishing 14 (February 1983): 155-61. An editor must remember
that the authors should have the last word on their manuscripts,
and that changes must be negotiated carefully. The two areas in
which an editor may take a strong stand are in deciding on the
kind of book that will be published and in selecting referees.
The editor should make his or her position on substantive editing
as forcefully as possible to the author, but should in the end be
willing to compromise. With all editing, "the editor proposes,
the author disposes."

Gross, Gerald, ed. Editors on Editing: An Inside View of What
Editors Really Do. New York: Harper and Row, revised edition
1985.

Montagnes, Ian. "Looking at the Last Dollar." Scholarly
Publishing 6 (October 1974): 33-39.

Woodford, F. Peter. "Training Professional Editors for Scientific
Journals." Scholarly Publishing 2 (October 1970): 41-46.

X

SCHOLARS AND TECHNOLOGY

"The First Decade of Personal Computing" by DAVID H.AHL.
Heath/Zenith Z-100 User's Guide by HUGH KENNER.
Directory of Online Databases from Cuadra Associates.
Microcomputer Market Place 1987 from R. R. Bowker.
"Databases for the Humanities" by JOSEPH RABEN.
The New Optical Media Mid-1986: A status Report, The New Optical
        Media in the Library and the Academy Tomorrow, and Moving
        Information: Graphic Images on CD ROM by DAVID C. MILLER.
"Optical Scanning: How It Helps, How It Works, and What It Costs"
        from Scholarly Communication.
The Electronic Scholar: A Guide to Academic Microcomputing
        by JOHN SHELTON LAWRENCE.
"A New Environment for Literary Analysis" by JOHN B. SMITH.
Machines Who Think by PAMELA McCORDUCK.
Computer Power and Human Reason: From Judgement to Calculation
        by JOSEPH WEIZENBAUM.

Related reading

"From Altair to AT" by WAYNE PARKER.
"10 Years of Byte: Special Anniversary Supplement" from Byte.
"Byte U. K.: Seventh Anniversary of Microcomputing"
        by DICK POUNTAIN.
"Byte Japan: A History of Japan's Microcomputers"
        by WILLIAM M. RAIKE.
A Grin on the Interface: Word Processing for the Academic Humanist
        by ALAN T. McKENZIE.
The Scholar's Personal Computing Handbook: A Practical Guide
        by BRYAN PFAFFENBERGER.
Writing with a Word Processor by WILLIAM ZINSSER.
The North America Online Directory from R. R. Bowker.
The Software Encyclopedia 1986/87 from R. R. Bowker.
Data Bases in the Humanities and Social Sciences
        edited by THOMAS F. MOBERG.
Sixth International Conference on Computers and the Humanities
        edited by SARAH K. BURTON and DOUGLAS D. SHORT.
Compact Disc Interactive: An Early 1987 Status Report
        by DAVID C. MILLER.
"CD ROM: The Little Leviathan" by REED McMANUS.
"The New Papyrus: CD ROM in Your Library?" by TINA ROOSE.
PC Magazine special issue on optical scanning.
"Page-to-Disk Technology: Nine State-of-the-Art Scanners"
        by TOM STANTON, DIANE BURNS, and S. VENIT.
A Guide to Computer Applications in the Humanities
        by SUSAN HOCKEY.

"ARTFL: A New Tool for French Studies"
        by ALICE McLEAN, ROBERT MORRISSEY, and DONALD ZIFF.
Turing's Man: Western Culture in the Computer Age
        by J. DAVID BOLTER.
The Second Self: Computers and the Human Spirit by SHERRY TURKLE.
The Information Technology Revolution edited by TOM FORESTER.
"Technology and Responsibility: Reflections on the New Tasks of
        Ethics" by HANS JONAS.
The Culture of Technology by ARNOLD PACEY.
"Nature and Conditions of Social Science" by MARC J. ROBERTS.

AHL, DAVID H. "The First Decade of Personal Computing." Creative Computing 10 (November 1984): 30-45.

In 1974 the personal computer industry consisted of a small group of engineers, often self-taught, working in garages and spare back rooms; yet, by 1984 it was a multi-million dollar industry led by one of the major U.S. corporations, IBM, and an enterprising newcomer, Apple. David Ahl gives a nostalgic and anecdotal account of this incredible growth in the ten-year anniversary issue of Creative Computing. The article is well written and nontechnical.

Ahl describes some of the landmarks that shaped this new industry: the first integrated computer (the Sphere in 1975); the development of faster, more powerful microprocessing units; the creation of the Apple I in 1976; the transition from kits to packaged systems with the arrival the Apple II, the Commodore Pet, and the RTS-80 in 1977; the entry of venture capitalists in the late 70's; and the arrival of the IBM PC in 1981.

The article captures the pioneering spirit of the early years in the industry and touches briefly on the factors that led to the personal computer's rise as a basic tool for business, education, and research. Emphasizing description rather than analysis, the article is excellent for the reader who wants a feel for how the industry was born and its early development but does not need a detailed analysis of the factors underlying the industry's evolution.

Ahl is the founder and editor of Creative Computing which ceased publication in 1986.

Related reading

Parker, Wayne. "From Altair to AT." PC World (March 1985): 78-88.

Byte. "10 Years of Byte: Special Anniversary Supplement." Byte 10 (September 1985): 197-222.

Pountain, Dick. "Byte U.K.: Seventh Anniversary of Microcomputing." Byte 10 (September 1985): 385-92.

Raike, William M. "Byte Japan: A History of Japan's Microcomputers." Byte 10 (September 1985): 395-99.

KENNER, HUGH. <u>Heath/Zenith Z-100 User's Guide</u>. Bowie, Maryland: Brady Communications Company, Inc., 1984.

The title of this book is misleading: while Hugh Kenner uses a Zenith computer, the book is an excellent guide for the new user of any type of computer whether it operates under an MS-DOS or CP/M system. In an easily-read, entertaining style, Kenner makes the computer understandable and manageable.

He begins with the fundamentals--the parts that make up the computer and the information the reader needs to know to begin computing. He goes on to explain how computers operate, why there are different programming languages, how software works, and the uses of wordprocessing, spread sheet, and database software programs. By the end of three short lessons in BASIC the reader will have written a very useful program and have a rudimentary understanding of how computers are programmed.

Less than two hundred pages in length, the Guide both provides the information necessary to begin using a computer effectively and establishes a good foundation for further exploration of the computer's capability.

Hugh Kenner is a Professor of English at The Johns Hopkins University.

Related reading

McKenzie, Alan T. ed. <u>A Grin on the Interface: Word Processing for the Academic Humanist</u>. New York: The Modern Language Association, 1984.

Pfaffenberger, Bryan. <u>The Scholar's Personal Computing Handbook: A Practical Guide</u>. Boston: Little, Brown and Company, 1986. A more detailed guide with excellent references.

Zinsser, William. <u>Writing with a Word Processor</u>. New York: Harper and Row, 1983.

<u>Directory of Online Databases</u>.   Santa Monica: Cuadra Associates, quarterly.

R.R. BOWKER.   <u>Microcomputer Market Place 1987</u>.   New York: R.R. Bowker, 1987.

Designed for libraries, businesses, and other microcomputer users, the Directory of Online Databases lists databases available through online service organizations connected to national and international telecommunications networks.   Listing more than 2500 databases from over 350 online vendors, the directory includes information on the type of database and subjects covered, geographical and chronological coverage, frequency of updating, the name and address of the database producer, the online service through which it is available, and the conditions of database use.

Databases are indexed by name, subject, database producer, online service, and telecommunications network.   A Master index covers all likely ways of identification including alternate names and acronyms.

The Directory is updated every six months and is available quarterly by subscription.   The four issues each year consist of two complete reissues of the directory and two issues of the update supplement.

R.R. Bowker's <u>Microcomputer Marketplace 1987</u> is a comprehensive directory of more than 23,000 organizations in all areas of the microcomputer industry.   The directory lists manufacturers and distributors of microcomputers, peripherals, and supplies; software publishers and distributors; microcomputer periodicals; associations representing all aspects of the industry; CD-ROM manufacturers; companies that provide special computer services; and computer conferences, meetings, and expositions.

The directory makes it easy to locate companies that offer specific computing products or services.   This is an update and expansion of an earlier publication by R.R. Bowker.

Related reading

R.R. Bowker.   <u>The North American Online Directory</u>.   New York: R.R. Bowker, 1987.   Lists more than 2,400 databases and discusses 1,500 companies that provide databases and online services.

R.R. Bowker.   <u>The Software Encyclopedia 1986/87</u>.   New York: R.R. Bowker, 1987.   A listing of over 28,000 programs from more than 3600 software producers.   The programs are listed alphabetically and by hardware compatibility.

RABEN, JOSEPH. "Databases for the Humanities." Scholarly Publishing 18 (October 1986): 23-28.

One of the consequences of the increased use of personal computers by humanists has been the proliferation of databases of interest to humanistic research. Many of these databases are the residue of individual research projects, often concordances. Others are special database projects such as the Thesaurus Linguae Graecae, containing Greek texts from about 750 B. C. to 600 A. D., or the Trésor de la Langue Française, a collection of about 1600 machine-readable French texts from the eighteenth through the twentieth century which was begun as a comprehensive dictionary of the French language. (The Thesaurus Linguae Graecae is annotated in section IX.)

Raben discusses many of these databases as well as projects designed to organize and catalogue textual materials available in machine-readable form. He points out that the use of such databases inevitably will alter the way researchers interact with their research materials. It is now possible for scholars to search for particular words and phrases, or even relationships among words or phrases, in one work or a collection of works in a very short time. Raben points that this allows closer and more extensive examination of texts. He notes, too, that computer-based research techniques help scholars evaluate more completely the interpretations of their predecessors.

The increased availability of computer databases, coupled with the enthusiastic adoption of computer methods by younger scholars, promises to alter the way researchers interact with their data. Raben states that it is too early to know what new interpretations this mode of scholarship will produce, but he predicts the outcome will be a result of the creative pairing of technical developments and human imagination. One technological advance that will have a major impact on database use is the advent of CD-ROM with its ability to store and provide access to video materials as well as text and sound.

Raben describes the growth of other computer services available to humanists including networks linking scholars and the increased number of conferences devoted in whole or in part to computer-related issues.

Raben is director of Paradigm Press, Osprey, Florida.

Related reading

Moberg, Thomas F. Data Bases in the Humanities and Social Sciences. Osprey, Florida: Paradigm Press, 1987. Papers presented at the fifth International Conference on Data Bases in the Humanities and Social Sciences, Grinnell College, June 1985.

Burton, Sarah K. and Douglas D. Short, eds. Sixth International Conference on Computers and the Humanities. Rockville, Maryland: Science Press, Inc., 1983. A collection of papers on computer applications in the humanities.

MILLER, DAVID C. The New Optical Media Mid-1986: A Status Report, The New Optical Media in the Library and the Academy Tomorrow, and Moving Information: Graphic Images on CD ROM. Benicia, California: DCM Associates, 1986.

These three reports on optical disk technology, prepared for the Fred Meyer Charitable Trust, provide excellent summaries of the state of optical disk technology in the mid 1980s and its relevance to the academic world. Miller describes the various types of optical media available: compact music disks, compact disks with read only memory (CD-ROMs), disks that are purchased blank but can be written on once, and interactive disks, and discusses their limitations and appropriate use. Miller also looks at three optical storage formats--disks, cards, and film-- and the equipment necessary to gain access to optically stored data.

In the final report, Miller discusses the problems encountered when graphic images are stored on optical media. He cites the advantages and disadvantages of storage formats and describes the difference between digital and analog recording.

The reports are well written and contain a wealth of basic information on optical storage technology for the novice in this area.

Miller is a business and technology consultant.

Related reading

Miller, David C. Compact Disc Interactive: An Early 1987 Status Report. Benicia, California: DCM Associates, 1987.

McManus, Reed. "CD ROM: The Little Leviathan" PC World (October 1986): 272.

Roose, Tina. "The New Papyrus: CD ROM in Your Library?" Library Journal 111 (September 1, 1986): 166.

Office of Scholarly Communication and Technology. "Optical Scanning: How it Helps, How it Works, and What it Costs." Scholarly Communication no. 2 (Fall 1985): 1-2.

Transferring textual materials into computer-readable form is a major problem for many researchers in the humanities who use computer analysis in their research. Optical scanning, a technique in which a machine "reads" the text and translates it into the corresponding bits and bytes, would seem to be the ideal solution. However, optical scanners are still in the early stages of development and almost all of those that are within a scholar's budget can only read clearly typewritten nonproportional texts.

"Optical Scanning" describes how optical scanners work and discusses how a scanner was used in the preparation of a special edition of the works of Thomas Carlyle. Three to four editions of each Carlyle volume were collated and compared in preparing the edition, a feat that would have been difficult if not impossible without the use of a scanner.

The article discusses the versatile but expensive Kurzweil scanner that was used in the Carlyle project in some detail and mentions several currently available scanners that are more moderately priced.

Related reading

PC Magazine (July 9, 1985). Special issue on optical scanners. A number of articles give a history of the scanner, summarize the current state and future of scanning technology, and discuss in detail the Kurzweil scanner and other less expensive alternatives.

Stanton, Tom, Diane Burns, and S. Venit. "Page-to-Disk Technology: Nine State-of-the-Art Scanners," PC Magazine (September 30, 1986): 128-77. An update on improvements in optical scanning technology.

LAWRENCE, JOHN SHELTON.   The Electronic Scholar: A Guide to
Academic Microcomputing.   Norwood, N.J.: Ablex Publishing
Corporation, 1984.

Most academic scholars have access to personal computers, but
few know how to make the best use of these machines in their
academic work.   The Electronic Scholar was written to show how
computers can most effectively assist scholars in research,
instruction, and administrative tasks.

Assuming the reader knows how to use a computer, Lawrence
addresses such issues as how to choose the word processing program
most appropriate to a scholar's style of writing, the use of
computers and electronic communication in collaborative and team
writing, electronic filing, searching for information both in the
user's own electronic files and from computer-based information
sources, and the use of electronics in publishing manuscripts.   A
final chapter on the legal and social issues involved in using
computers and electronic media discusses some of the more complex
and troublesome aspects of this new technology.   Lawrence
describes many concrete computer applications and some appropriate
hardware and software programs.   He also provides an extensive
bibliography at the end of each chapter.

Lawrence is a faculty member at Morningside College in Sioux
City, Iowa.

Related reading

Hockey, Susan.   A Guide to Computer Applications in the
Humanities.   Baltimore: The Johns Hopkins University Press, 1980.
This is a more detailed description of the use of computers in
humanities research, particularly in languages and literature
projects, using main frame computers.

SMITH, JOHN B. "A New Environment for Literary Analysis."
Perspectives in Computing 4 (Summer/Fall 1984): 20-31.

John Smith has developed a computer program called ARRAS that
allows fast, flexible, open-ended analysis of individual texts.
Although applied to literary analysis in this article, it can
analyze texts on any subject: literature, history, government, or
business. Smith notes, "the functions that perform a thematic
analysis of a literary work can also locate all passages in an
[environmental] impact statement in which specific combinations of
ideas are discussed."

The program has three major components: a collection of texts
in machine-readable form, internal self-instruction that makes it
easy for even a beginner to use, and a system for text retrieval
and analysis. Smith emphasizes that ARRAS is not a "black box,"
into which one inserts a text and a few instructions and then
receives a completed analysis. Instead, ARRAS should be thought
of as a toolbox with each tool designed for a particular task. It
"amplifies, rather than replaces, specific perceptual and
cognitive functions" of the user. It is the user who decides what
information is important, what direction the analysis should take,
and what the outcome means.

The analysis system, among other capabilities, allows ARRAS
to display each occurrence of a word, of categories of words, or
of combinations of words or categories. It also can display a
distribution of words, categories, or combinations in specified
intervals of text. Although the article describes the use of
ARRAS on a mainframe computer, a version called MICROARRAS is
available for use on personal computers.

Smith notes that one of the program's advantages is that it
helps scholars alter the linear point of view inherent in the
temporal nature of reading a text. In its analysis, ARRAS looks
down on the entire text at once, allowing the user a different
sense of analytical precision: assuring that any analysis includes
all occurrences of words, themes, or patterns. ARRAS also allows
users to trace historical development over a large database of
texts, by showing patterns, themes, stylistic traits, grammatical
forms, and other features in a longitudinal way.

Smith is an associate professor in the Department of Computer
Science, University of North Carolina at Chapel Hill.

Related reading

McLean, Alice, Robert Morrissey, and Donald Ziff. "ARTFL: A New
Tool for French Studies." Scholarly Communication no. 8 (Summer
1987): 1, 6-9. A discussion of American and French Research on
the Treasury of the French Language (ARTFL), a French and American
project for retrieving and analyzing data contained in Trésor de
la Langue Française, a computerized dictionary of the French
language. This database is similar in many respects to the
Thesaurus Linguae Graecae annotated in section IX. The database
can be retrieved and analyzed using ARRAS.

McCORDUCK, PAMELA. <u>Machines Who Think</u>. New York: W. H. Freeman and Company, 1979.

An oft-quoted classic in computer literature, this book traces the conception and development of artificial intelligence from Charles Babbage's analytical engine through the chemical analysis and medical diagnostic programs of the late 1970s. McCorduck looks at a technological subject through humanistic eyes using biographical sketches of the key workers and placing the evolution of artificial intelligence in an historical and cultural framework.

Woven throughout the work is a thoughtful discussion of the philosophical and psychological factors that make most of us, including some computer scientists, uncomfortable with the idea of machines programmed to be more intelligent than humans.

The book concludes with a reflection on the moral and ethical dimensions of artificial intelligence and speculation on the direction of artificial intelligence in the future.

McCorduck is the author of numerous articles and books on artificial intelligence.

Related reading

Bolter, J. David. <u>Turing's Man: Western Culture in the Computer Age</u>. Chapel Hill, North Carolina: The University of North Carolina Press, 1984.

Turkle, Sherry. <u>The Second Self: Computers and the Human Spirit</u>. New York: Simon and Schuster, 1984.

Forester, Tom, ed. <u>The Information Technology Revolution</u>. Cambridge, Massachusetts: MIT Press, 1985.

WEIZENBAUM, JOSEPH. <u>Computer Power and Human Reason: From Judgement to Calculation</u>. New York: W. H. Freeman and Company, 1976.

The current fascination with computers has led many technically-oriented thinkers to try to interpret almost everything, including human behavior and society, in the image of computers. Simultaneously, technologists are pushing the computer far beyond its present tasks--complex mathematical calculations and manipulation of large amounts of data and textual material-- into such unexplored areas as artificial intelligence--machines that can replace and extend human intelligence--and machines that can recognize human speech.

In <u>Computer Power and Human Reason</u> Joseph Weizenbaum points out the hazards of continuing to allow technology to develop and be used without the intervention of human reason and moral judgement. He warns against the dangers inherent in pursuing any type of computer application just because it is technically feasible. His message is as pertinent today as when he wrote in more than a decade ago.

While this important book focuses on the computer, it applies as well to the dangers of overenthusiastically pursuing any technology whose advancing capabilities outstride the ethical and philosophical deliberations necessary to insure the technology will be used for the common good.

The message of the book comes mainly from the first and last two or three chapters. Many of those in between, while interesting, are quite technical and difficult to follow and are not necessary to comprehend the author's point.

Weizenbaum is professor of computer science at the Massachusetts Institute of Technology.

Related reading

Jonas, Hans. "Technology and Responsibility: Reflections on the New Tasks of Ethics" <u>Social Research</u> 40 (Spring 1973): 31-54.

Pacey, Arnold. <u>The Culture of Technology</u>. Cambridge, Massachusetts: MIT Press, 1983. Pacey argues that technology is not value-free and that its development and use depends both on human inventiveness and on the culture into which it is introduced.

Roberts, Marc J. "Nature and Condition of Social Science" <u>Daedalus</u> 103 (Summer 1974): 47-64.

XI

PUBLIC POLICY: COPYRIGHT, FUNDING, ACCESS

Intellectual Property Rights in an Age of Electronics and
      Information from U.S. Congress,
      Office of Technology Assessment.
"Copyright Can Survive the New Technologies" by DENNIS D.
      McDONALD.
"Impact from U.S. Government Printing on Public Access to
      Government Information"
      by PETER HERNON and CHARLES R. McCLURE.
"Who Will Have the Numbers? The Rise of the Statistical Services
      Industry and the Politics of Public Data"
      by PAUL STARR and ROSS CORSON.
"Federal Restrictions on the Free Flow of Academic Information and
      Ideas" by JOHN SHATTUCK.

Related reading

General Guide to the Copyright Act of 1976
      by U.S. Copyright Office, Library of Congress.
"Fair Use Versus Fair Return"
      by IRVING LOUIS HOROWITZ and MARY E. CURTIS.
"Publishers, Technological Change, and Copyright: Maintaining the
      Balance" by MEREDITH A. BUTLER.
"Software, Libraries & the Copyright Law"
      by SUSAN S. LYTLE and HAL W. HALL.
"A Publisher's Guide to the New U. S. Copyright Law"
      by SANFORD G. THATCHER.
"Restricting Information: National Security Versus Rights of
      Citizens" by GEORGE E. BROWN, JR.
"Information:" Public or Private?" by JEAN SMITH.
"The Commercialization and Privatization of Government
      Information" by DIANE SMITH.
"Editorial: The Right of Access to Information"
      by RICHARD DOUGHERTY.
"The Financing and Governance of Information Networks of the
      Future: The Private Sector" by PAUL ZURKOWSKI.
Electronic Collection and Dissemination of Information by Federal
      Agencies: A Policy Overview
      by the House Committee on Government Operations.

133

U.S. Congress, Office of Technology Assessment. <u>Intellectual Property Rights in an Age of Electronics and Information</u>. OTA-CIT-302. Washington: Government Printing Office, April 1986.

This report examines the impact of recent and anticipated advances in communication and information technologies on the intellectual property system. It focuses primarily on the Federal copyright system, and on the continuing effectiveness of copyright law as a policy tool in the light of technologies such as audio and videorecorders, computer programs, electronic databases, and telecommunications networks.

To obtain a comprehensive view, the study examined the intellectual property system from a number of perspectives: the constitutional basis of intellectual property policy; the system's goals, laws and economics; the creative environment; problems of enforcement; the international context; and the Federal role in administering intellectual property rights.

OTA found that technological developments are affecting all aspects of the intellectual property system. Moreover, because we are only beginning to move into the era of electronic information, the full impact of new technologies will not become apparent for some time. Fundamental changes are occurring in information technologies that will antiquate many of the policy mechanisms now in force, and bring new intellectual property problems requiring new solutions. Thus, even if Congress acts now in response to current problems, it will need to be prepared to act again within the next decade.

Related reading

Library of Congress, U. S. Copyright Office. <u>General Guide to the Copyright Act of 1976</u>. Washington: Government Printing Office, September 1979.

Horowitz, Irving Louis and Mary E. Curtis. "Fair Use Versus Fair Return: Copyright Legislation and its Consequences." <u>Journal of the American Society for Information Science</u> 35 (March 1984): 67-74.

McDONALD, DENNIS D. "Copyright Can Survive the New Technologies." <u>Bulletin of the American Society for Information Science</u> 10 (1983-1984): 19-22.

Copyright protects a creative work that has been put into tangible form. "It protects the form in which ideas are embodied, not the ideas themselves." The greatest threat to copyright comes from recent technological advances, which make it easy to copy a copyrighted work without the knowledge of the copyright holder. New forms also make it difficult to determine exactly what is copyrighted. An example is a database that is continually updated, never becoming fixed in a tangible form.

McDonald raises two additional questions: how payments should be made; and whether the copyright owner has control over the circumstances of copying. He evaluates alternative methods for payment (taxing copying equipment and distributing the proceeds on the basis of a sampling, and price discrimination). McDonald urges writers, artists, and producers to speak out strongly to the public about the value of copyright.

McDonald is vice president of King Research, Inc. Rockville, Maryland.

Related reading

Butler, Meredith A. "Publishers, Technological Change, and Copyright: Maintaining the Balance." <u>Drexel Library Qarterly</u> 20 (Summer 1984): 28-41. The publisher, librarian, educator, author, and user communities remain sharply divided over what constitutes acceptable and fair use of copyright materials. Major actors in the debate are the American Library Association, the Association of American Publishers, and the Information Industry Association, each speaking for its own large constituency. Butler describes their positions, the outlook for additional legislation, and the progress of copyright litigation, providing a convenient summary of recent events. She observes that what is needed is a new conceptual framework for examining the conflicts--a "coherent information/communication policy founded on the idea of intellectual property." This even-handed review of the difficult and value-laden copyright questions provides a good foundation for understanding the participants' major concerns.

Lytle, Susan S. and Hal W. Hall. "Software, Libraries & the Copyright Law." <u>Library Journal</u> 110 (July 1985): 33-39.

Thatcher, Sanford G. "A Publisher's Guide to the New U.S. Copyright Law." <u>Scholarly Publishing</u> 8 (July 1977): 315-33. This synopsis of the 1976 U.S. Copyright Law from the publisher's perspective is particularly useful because it is organized according to categories of works (the law is not). The author has a concluding note on infringement of copyright and its prevention.

HERNON, PETER and CHARLES R. McCLURE "Impact from U.S. Government Printing on Public Access to Government Information," Drexel Library Quarterly 20 (Summer 1984): 42-62.

Hernon and McClure review one of the most highly politicized issues today: freedom of access to information. Of most concern are federal government policies and activities affecting dissemination of government information, copyright, transborder data flow, and commercialization of information resources and services. The Reagan administration has endorsed the view that information is a resource of economic value that deserves to be treated as such and that the government should rely as much as possible on commercial sources for information. Publishing activities have been severely curtailed throughout the government. The costs of producing and disseminating information have been given precedence over the responsiblility to make it available to taxpayers. In addition, the administration has endorsed higher classification levels for government documents, and funding cuts that restrict library collections and services.

Related reading

The articles listed below provide background and perspectives on constraints on the flow of information. Brown, a Congressman from California, discusses actions by the Reagan administration. Jean Smith and Diane Smith speak from the perspective of documents librarians. Dougherty discusses the recent "Report of the Commission on Freedom and Equality of Access to Information," by an American Library Association committee and Zurkowski, president of the Information Industry Association, expresses the IIA position on these issues. (In addition, the Council on Library Resources and the Association of Research Libraries both have issued statements on access to information.)

Brown, George E., Jr. "Restricting Information: National Security Versus Rights of Citizens," Bulletin of the American Society for Information Science 8 (April 1982): 36.

Smith, Jean. "Information: Public or Private?" Special Libraries 75 (October 1984): 275-82.

Smith, Diane. "The Commercialization and Privatization of Government Information." Government Publications Review 12 (January-February 1985): 45-63.

Dougherty, Richard. "Editorial: The Right of Access to Information." Journal of Academic Librarianship 11 (September 1985): 195.

Zurkowski, Paul. "The Financing and Governance of Information Networks of the Future: The Private Sector," in Martha Boaz, Strategies for Meeting the Information Needs of Society in the Year 2000 (Littleton, Colo., Libraries Unlimited, 1981).

STARR, PAUL and ROSS CORSON. "Who Will Have the Numbers? The Rise of the Statistical Services Industry and the Politics of Public Data" in The Politics of Numbers, edited by William Alonso and Paul Starr. New York: Russell Sage Foundation, 1987.

Sociologists Paul Starr and Ross Corson look at the meteoric growth over the last twenty years of private statistical services and its implications for the availability of public information. The growing privatization of public data collection and dissemination, they argue, will limit the availability of information to the few who are able to pay for it and thus hamper the free flow of information so vital to social equity and well-being.

With the explosion of information in the past two decades-- largely a consequence of technological advances, cost reductions, and more widespread use of the computer--increasing numbers of independent companies have assumed, and are now competing for a greater share in, data gathering and processing activities traditionally reserved to the U.S. government.

Private firms are developing their own databases and offering clients such "data value-adding" services as time-sharing of computer models and facilities, "customized" data and professional consultation on data analysis. Business deregulation and technological innovation in the 1960s and 1970s led a wide variety of companies to enter into this new communication business. Recently such companies have begun objecting to public sector competition.

Complaining of unfair government pricing practices and of a supposed government monopoly in the information industry, private statistical services are seeking to cut back or eliminate government programs offering free or low-cost information to the public. And, according to the authors, they would like ultimately to restrict the government to producing and "wholesaling" raw data to the private sector.

Starr and Corson warn that the availability of information, if left to private retailers, would be determined by market considerations and not by public need. With cost-recovery rather than possible social gain as the principal criterion for data production and dissemination, the price of much of the public data now produced would increase substantially--placing it well out of reach of many potential users. Public data considered to be "unprofitable" would not be produced at all.

The authors point out that the marketplace approach does not account for the social benefits of cheap and easily accessible public information, much of which only the public sector is uniquely equipped to provide. Citing just a few of the myriad of societal activities and goals requiring freely available public statistics--medical research, higher education, political debate and economic reform--Storr and Corson give an eloquent and convincing defense for continued government investment and preeminence in information services.

SHATTUCK, JOHN. "Federal Restrictions on the Free Flow of
Academic Information and Ideas." <u>Government Information Quarterly</u>
3 (1986): 5-29.

The federal government recently has taken several actions and
formulated proposals that may erode the tradition of academic
freedom, usually justifying them by the need to protect national
security. Two areas are affected: the dissemination of ideas, and
access by foreign scholars to U.S. higher education facilities.

In the first category are requirements for prepublication
review of government sponsored university research, authorizing
secret classifications for research after the projects have begun,
and limiting the distribution of sensitive but unclassified
information via export controls.

Under the second category, foreign nationals are sometimes
denied entry to the U.S. or are deported because of their
political beliefs or ideologies. Speakers invited to address
university audiences have been denied entry as well. Shattuck
concludes that these policies are self-defeating, and that they
may inhibit innovation. He urges their reconsideration before
national values are compromised.

Shattuck is vice president for government, community, and
public afairs, Harvard University.

Related reading

House Committee on Government Operations. <u>Electronic Collection
and Dissemination of Information by Federal Agencies: A Policy
Overview</u>. Washington: House Report 99-560. 99th Congress, 2nd
session. April 29, 1986.

INDEX OF AUTHORS

INDEX OF AUTHORS

* Main entry

ABOUT THE AUTHORS

Herbert C. Morton was Director, Office of Scholarly
Communication and Technology, American Council of Learned
Societies, when this bibliography was prepared. Anne
J. Price was Staff Associate.

Jane Rosenberg was Program Associate, Council of
Library Resources. Deborah Styles was a free lance
editor. Carol Tenopir was Assistant Professor, School
of Library and Information Studies, University of Hawaii.
Bettina Hagen and Judith Mayers were members of the staff
of the Office of Scholarly Communication.